Marquart's Works

VOLUME III

CHURCH AND MINISTRY

Edited by
Herman J. Otten

LUTHERAN NEWS, INC., New Haven, Missouri

Marquart's Works

Library of Congress Card
Lutheran News, Inc.
684 Luther Lane
New Haven, MO 63068
Published 2014
Printed in the United States of America
Lightning Source, Inc., La Vergne, TN
ISBN #978-0-9644799-7-5

TABLE OF CONTENTS

FOREWORD

Dr. Marquart was a beloved Professor by all the students that sat in his classes. His ability to simplify great theological concepts made him a favorite Teacher for all the students who attended the Seminary. He not only instilled in us a love for Theology, but he also showed us how it was to be applied in a pastor's daily calling.

However, these writings are not just for pastors. Even dedicated laymen will be able to grasp and learn from this great Teacher of the Church. Whenever and wherever Dr. Marquart made a presentation, you would soon see that he was eagerly sought out, not just by pastors but also by laymen. They too recognized his genius in refuting those who denied the Word of God. He was as popular with laymen as he was with pastors. Here in these volumes you will once again be able to take your place and listen to this great Teacher, as he clearly enunciates various topics from a thoroughly Lutheran perspective. Since these multiple volumes consist of the various topics that Dr. Marquart addressed over his illustrious life, you will find it hard to put these volumes down.

Having Dr. Marquart's writings in book form will once again allow this fearless Champion of the Church to speak to the issues that continue to plague the Church from one generation to the next. False doctrine continues to be rehashed and sent out with new clothes. As the Proverb goes, "there is nothing new under the sun." Dr. Marquart had the remarkable ability to dissect what the issue was, and why it was, and still is, false doctrine. Confessional Lutherans from all over the world were always eager to attend Dr. Marquart's lectures. They recognized that he was a giant among men. Anyone concerned about the welfare of the Church will want to have these volumes on their bookshelf.

It appears that the Almighty Savior of the Church, in His infinite wisdom, chooses to send out only a few Teachers of the Church. One may make a very short list of these esteemed gifts from God. Luther, Chemnitz, Gerhard, Walther, Pieper, Preus, and Marquart. Their writings stand the test of time. These men did not write for some passing fad, that is here today and then blown away by tomorrow's changing wind vane. Any pastor or layman, who has a desire and love for the Truth, will not be disappointed with these volumes. Every congregation that has a love for the Lord and His saving Gospel, would do well to purchase the writings from these Teachers of the Church. God had His good reasons for raising these men up and sending them out, and it would be wise for pastors and laymen to read, mark, learn and inwardly digest the writings of these great defenders of the Gospel.

Rev. Herman Otten is to be commended for publishing The Writings of Dr. Kurt Marquart. This may well be Rev. Otten's finest and most enduring contribution to the Church.

Rev. Ray R. Ohlendorf
Salem Lutheran Church
Taylorsville, NC
4th Sunday in Lent 201

Acknowledgements

Well Herman,

As usual you find yourself doing what *unsere beliebte Synode* should have done long ago. The fact that CPH has not already published a book of Kurt's writings is an absolute travesty. It is an indictment of the politics before theology which has destroyed the orthodoxy of the LCMS. Our Savior Lutheran Church will stand by you in the worthy project. Back in the dark days when Bohlmann and his supporters were after Robert Preus we published a number of Kurt's magnificent essays on Robert's behalf. Modern Missouri has never produced another theologian comparable to him either in confessional fidelity or eloquence. We are proud and eager to take part in this belated effort. "Gottes Wort Und Luthers Lehr Vergehet Nun Und Nimmermehr."

Larry White, Pastor
Our Saviour Lutheran Church
Houston, Texas

Thanks to Luke Otten for arranging the publication of these volumes and to Naomi Finck, John Eberhart, Natalie Hoerstkamp, and Mary Zastrow for type-setting.

Thanks to Grace Otten for recognizing the importance of publishing *Marquart's Works* ever since they first began appearing in *Christian News* more than 50 years ago. Thanks to Scott Meyer, "America's confessional Lutheran" lay historian and President of the Concordia Historical Institute whose appreciation of Marquart's works and encouragement helped make the publication of these volumes possible.

PREFACE

Dr. C. F. W. Walther, first president of The Lutheran Church-Missouri Synod, has been rightly referred to as "The American Luther." As the editor of a Christian weekly for 51 years, the undersigned has reviewed thousands of books. During all these years he has published the writings of many theologians. The index at the back of Volume V of the *Christian News Encyclopedia* lists the names of hundreds of theologians whose writings have appeared in *Christian News*. Some, like Kurt Marquart, were also good friends. Yet, the editor knows of no theologian who deserves the title "The International Lutheran" more than Kurt Marquart. The editor's wife, Grace, is a graduate of Concordia College, St. Paul Minnesota and Valparaiso University. There she studied under some prominent theologians who later became professors at Concordia Seminary, St. Louis and Seminex. In 1963 Grace Otten and Kurt Marquart were *CN*'s reporters at the Fourth Assembly of the Lutheran World Federation in Helsinki, Finland. Following the LWF Assembly she and the editor's brother, Walter, who knew Marquart for 54 years, accompanied him on a twenty city lecture tour in the U.S. Grace shares the editor's evaluation of Kurt Marquart. She helped make it possible together with Luke Otten, Ruth Rethemeyer, Mary Beth Otten, Kristina Bailey and the Missourian Publishing Company, Washington, Missouri, to get *Marquart's Legacy* published in 2006 not long after his death. The 76 page *Marquart's Legacy* is available from *Christian News* for $5.00. It includes photos of Marquart and family and information about two professionally made videos showing Marquart in action.

Marquart's Legacy begins with a brief biography of Kurt Marquart. Then follows "Remembrances of a Former Seminary Roommate," the editor of *Christian News*. Next comes "The Lasting Legacy of Kurt Marquart" as expressed by many who knew him well.

The appendixes list the writings and reports of Kurt Marquart which have appeared in 44 volumes of *Christian News* (1962-2006), *A Christian Handbook on Vital Issues*, the five volumes of the *Christian News Encyclopedia, Luther Today, What Would He Do or Say?* and *Crisis in Christendom-Seminex Ablaze*. The lasting legacy of a great theologian and genius like Kurt Marquart can best be found in his works. *CN* suggested in 2006 that the Lutheran Church-Missouri Synod's Concordia Publishing House should publish *Marquart's Works*.

The questions at the end of each section are included to make *Marquart's Works* helpful for study. In an age when faith in historic Christianity is declining in all of the major denominations, *Marquart's Works* can be used to encourage and strengthen faithful Christians and begin a 21st Century Reformation and 21st Century Formula of Concord by the 500th anniversary of the Reformation in 2017.

Herman Otten
Reformation, 2014

COUNCIL OF CHURCHES

Sir,—The comparison of the World Council of Churches with the United Nations (Chronicle, October 11) was rather apt, and argues not for but against the Council. Purpose of this letter is to take issue with the claim that "no church compromises its position by becoming a member."

The basis for the U.N. obviously is the very fact that there is a larger unit, the world, of which the several nations are subdivisions. Similarly, the basic assumption underlying the W.C.C. is that the several denominations are all more or less legitimate subdivisions, which together make-up the Church. My Synod, for one, cannot accept this theory. It holds that there are not many churches, but only one Church, and that this one Church is already a divinely given fact, not an ideal still to be realized by men. This one Church is, according to Scripture and Creed, the Communion of Saints, the fellowship of all Christians in Christ. Since only genuine faith makes one a member of the Church, the Church is not a visible, external, empirical, statistical-sociological magnitude at all. Rather, the Church is not a visible, external. Rather, the Church is the mystical Body of Christ, which, although it truly exists here on earth, is perceived not by sight, but by faith alone. And faith can grasp the Church only in its external, objective marks, the pure Word and Sacraments.

This immediately raises the question of truth. Now, a secular U.N. concerns itself with questions of power. Yet even here it should not be assumed as self-evident that every nation must join. On the contrary, thoughtful observers put some searching questions: Why should nations which represent Western civilization—even granting its senile morbidities—put themselves on the same level with African cannibal tribes or worse, with Red barbarians, who spit upon all that is dear to civilized humanity? When a gentleman is forced to deal with a scoundrel, can he ever do that on terms of equality and cordially? Quod licet Jovi, non licet bovi! Is it a favor to the captive nations, when their oppressors are accorded ceremonial legitimacy in the West, instead of being branded as the international criminal gang they are?

Perhaps these ambiguities can be borne politically, in the U.N., where all moralities and immoralities have equal rights, and no common court of appeals, such as the basic moral-legal principles of the civilized community, is recognized. But under no circumstances can this skepticism, relativism, nihilism be tolerated in the field of religion, where not questions of power but questions of truth have life-or-death significance. To play U.N. here is simply disastrous.

It is precisely in order to keep the issue of truth alive, that we, for example, must shun an "Ecumenical Movement" which speaks and acts as if (1) The Church were the visible agglomerate or sum total of all denominations, and (2) truth were still uncertain, still to be arrived at through mutual discussions. Christ founded not a debating club, but a teaching Church, whose task is not to seek or discover but to proclaim the saving truth, and which therefore distinguishes sharply between truth and error, right and wrong (St. Matt. 28:20; Rom. 16:17; Gal. 1:8; and 9).

A Confessional Synod, conscious of representing the Faith of the one, holy Church of Christ cannot give the appearance of conferring legitimacy upon organizations disloyal to the Faith. And how can a confessional Synod belong to a "fellowship" (!) which claims and implies some sort of oneness in Christ (in other words, not a mere discussion—forum), while it tolerates in its midst and among its leaders public denial of such essentials of the Faith as the doctrines of the Holy Trinity, the Incarnation, the Redemption, the Inspiration of Scripture, the Sacraments, etc.? What sort of "good things" can be accomplished by combining faith and unbelief, truth and heresy, contrary to express divine command, II Cor. 6:14 ff? And what sort of lovely brotherly feeling can be expected to unite Christians with Communist-controlled "church-men," who have publicly applauded the butchers of Hungary, for example? How can anyone seriously speak here of mutual "correction of one another in Christ?"

No thank you!

K. Marquart

Toowoomba Chronicle and Darling Dows Gazette, October 14, 1961
Christian News, March 11, 1963

1. The one Church according to Scripture is ____.
2. The Church is not a ____.
3. Is it a favor to the captive nations when ____.
4. Why should true Christians shun the "Ecumenical Movement?" ____.
5. Christ did not found a ____ club, but a ____ a teaching ____.
6. What sort of good thing can be accomplished by combining ____ and ____?

THE MARKS OF THE CHURCH - ESSAY

I. The Need for MARKS OF THE CHURCH

God's Church on earth consists of all Christians, and only of Christians (Rom. 8:9; 12:5; Eph. 1: 23; 2:20,21; 5:30; 1 Pet. 2 : 5). And the Christians are all those, and only those, in whom the Spirit of God, through Word and Sacrament, has created and still sustains that faith which both lays hold on the alone-saving merit or righteousness of Christ (justification), and produces love and good works (sanctification), and which therefore is the very essence of spiritual life.

Faith alone, then, makes one a member of Christ's Church. He who has faith is a member of the Church, no matter to what time, place, race, nation, or denomination he belong. On the other hand, he who lacks this faith, or has lost it, does not belong to the Church, even though he be baptized, confirmed, and ordained, have his name registered on a congregational membership list, or perhaps even be prominent or hold office in a congregation or synod!

Faith, however, cannot be seen by men, since we human beings cannot look into each other's hearts—that is God's prerogative! It follows, since faith alone determines one's membership in the Church, that the Church, as such, is invisible to human eyes. Its true membership is known to God alone, Rom. 11:4; 2 Tim. 2:19. Therefore Dr. Martin Luther wrote:—

> This item: "I believe one holy Christian Church," is just as much an article of faith as are the others. Therefore no reason, even if it put on all its spectacles, can recognize her. The devil can indeed cover her up with offenses and divisions, so that you should take offense. Thus also God can hide her beneath weaknesses and all sorts of deficiencies, so that you must become a fool over it all, and form a wrong judgment concerning her. She wishes not to be seen, but to be believed; but faith deals with what one does not see, Heb. 11, 1. *(Preface to Revelation.)*

Or, even more severely:—

> The holy Church of Christ speaks thus; I believe one holy Christian Church; the mad Church of the Pope speaks thus: I see one holy Christian Church. *(Reply to Emser.)*

But this creates a difficulty: If the real Church of Christ is invisible, then where and how and by what means can we find her, or have anything to do with her? Obviously, unless the whole thing is to dissolve into the very thin air of impractical theory, there must be some very down-to-earth, visible, tangible signs or evidences, by means of which the presence of the Church can be recognized; in short, there must be *marks of the Church!*

There is yet another problem which dramatizes the need for *marks of the Church:*

One often hears—especially when men are faced with confessional decisions, that is, when they are reminded that consistent Christians are not permitted to have religious fellowship with groups or churches which

3

depart in some way from God's pure Word and Sacraments—comments along these lines: "But, Pastor, there are so many hundreds of churches in the world, each claiming to be the true one, and each regarding the others as false! How can we tell which, if any, of them is true?"

At least four comments should be made at this point:—

1. The basic choices among churches are very, very few. Disregarding such obviously non-Christian, fanatical modern cults as Christian Science or Jehovah's Witnesses, the choices are about as follows: The first basic choice is between Roman Catholicism (or the very similar Eastern Orthodoxy) and Protestantism. If one decides that Rome cannot be right, then one is again faced with a basic choice between the two kinds of Protestantism, Lutheran and Reformed. All the non-Lutheran Protestant churches of to-day have grown out of the Reformed branch of the tree. Therefore the Lutheran Church should be contrasted not individually with every other denomination, like the Church of England, the Methodists, the Baptists, and the like, but collectively with all of these taken together; for all non-Lutheran Protestant churches form one single Reformed camp. All of them, without exception, officially deny, for example, the Lutheran doctrine of the Real Presence of the body and blood of Christ in the holy Sacrament of the Altar. And the divisions *within* the Reformed camp are mainly not about doctrine, but about forms of church-government, some insisting on bishops, others on a Presbyterian, and still others on a congregational form of government. Doctrinally, the choices are not very many indeed!

2. Contrary to popular belief, most churches today do *not* believe that they are right, and everybody else is wrong. The vast majority of Protestant churches to-day are confused about doctrine, and therefore act on the principle of "live and let live". The general mood is, at least among the leadership: "We have our beliefs, and you have yours. Let us not condemn one another as wrong. On the points of doctrine which divide us, no one can really be sure. Different doctrines are simply different aspects of the same truth. Therefore let us get together." The result of this attitude is the Ecumenical Movement, which includes both the World Council of Churches and the Lutheran World Federation. The only reason why there is an Ecumenical Movement is that the churches are **not** sure of the truth. If they were, the Movement would fall to pieces. But if men believe not that they **have** the truth, but that they are merely *looking for it,* then why should they not look for it together? Many heads are better than few!

To cite but one example, there is "The Faith of the Church", a recently (1959) issued document, prepared by official representatives of the Congregational, Methodist and Presbyterian Churches in Australia, and suggested as a basis upon which these three churches are to merge into one united body. According to their representatives, the three merging churches do not believe that they have the right doctrine:

"We none of us come into union expressing the Church's Faith in its fullness, but confessing to God and one another the partial character of our vision, the **confusion of our preaching**, the poverty of our wor-

4

ship, and the weakness of our fellowship. . . . There is a given Faith, but we do not yet know it in its fullness; we have not spoken of it as we ought." (p. 29, our dark-type emphasis.)

"We are none of us asked to subscribe to what have been the distinctive theological emphasis of another; nor are we entitled, any of us, to claim that we come in the fullness of the Faith." (p. 32.)

Nor—naturally! The stream cannot rise higher than its source!—will the new church, resulting from the proposed merger, claim that its doctrine is really God-given and true:

"We suggest that the Church in any given time or place is incapable of articulating the Faith in its fullness . . ." (p. 32).

"No system of doctrine . . . is sufficiently free from error to be permitted to hold anything but a subordinate position in the life of the Christian Church." (p. 41.)

3. This modern confusion and doubt clearly demonstrate the dreadful curse of false doctrine: The more error multiplies, the more it makes men uncertain of everything, even the truth! Finally men throw up their hands in despair, and ask with Pontius Pilate: "What is truth?"

In a sense, however, the doctrinal confusion in the major Protestant sects renders much easier the task of him who sincerely seeks the true visible Church; for he can immediately dismiss all churches which are not certain of their doctrine. Only a Church which speaks and acts with conviction and authority and is capable of distinguishing sharply between truth and error, right and wrong, can possibly represent *Christ, Who founded not a debating society for the **discovery** of truth, but a teaching Church for the **preaching** and **proclamation** of truth!* Christ and all His holy Apostles claimed to represent, and commanded the Church to represent, not weak and uncertain human guesses, opinions or theories about the truth, but the final, certain divine truth itself; "teaching them to observe all things whatsoever I have commanded you," Matt. 28 : 20; "If ye continue in my word, then are ye my disciples indeed; and ye shall know the truth, and the truth shall make you free," John 8 : 31-32; "I have not shunned to declare unto you all the counsel of God," Acts 20:27; "Mark them which cause divisions and offenses contrary to the doctrine which ye have learned, and avoid them," Rom. 16 : 17; "If the trumpet give an uncertain sound, who shall prepare himself to the battle?" 1 Cor. 14.8; "If any man preach any other gospel unto you than that ye have received, let him be accursed," Gal. 1:9; "Hold fast the form of sound words, which thou hast heard of us. . . . Study to show thyself approved unto God, a workman that needeth not to be ashamed, rightly dividing the word of truth. . . . For men shall be . . . ever learning, and never able to come to the knowledge of the truth. . . But thou hast fully known my doctrine . . . continue thou in the things which thou hast learned and hast been assured of, knowing of whom thou hast learned them," 2 Tim. 1:13; 2:15; 3:2, 7, 10, 14; " A bishop must be blameless . . . holding fast the faithful word as he hath been taught, that he may be able by sound doctrine both to exhort and to convince the gainsayers . . . in doctrine shewing uncorruptness. . . .

5

These things speak, and exhort, and rebuke with all authority. Let no man despise thee." Tit. 1:7, 8; 2:7, 15; " If any man speak, let him speak as the oracles of God," 1 Pet. 4:11; "Ye should earnestly contend for the faith which was once delivered unto the saints," Jude 3.

This is also the spirit of the great Reformer, Dr. Martin Luther, who wrote, against Erasmus:

"The Holy Spirit is no Skeptic, and the things He has written in our hearts are not doubts or opinions, but assertions—surer and more certain than sense and life itself." *(The Bondage of the Will.)*

And elsewhere Luther says: "Whatever wavers or doubts, that cannot be truth. And what would be the use or need of a Church of God in the world, if she would waver and be uncertain in her words, or propose something new every day, now give this, now take that? . . . Doctrine. . . does not belong into the Our Father when we pray. Forgive us our debts! For doctrine is not of our doing, but it is God's own Word, Who cannot sin nor do wrong. For a preacher must not pray the Our Father, nor seek forgiveness of sins, when he has preached (if he is a true preacher), but he must say and boast with Jeremiah, Jer. 17, 16: "Lord, Thou knowest, that out of my mouth hath gone forth that which is right and pleasing to Thee," yea, he must defiantly say with St. Paul and all Apostles and Prophets: *Haec dixit Dominus*, This God Himself has said. And again: I have been an Apostle and Prophet of Jesus Christ in this sermon. Here it is not necessary, yea not good, to ask for forgiveness of sin, as if it were taught wrongly; for it is God's and not my word, which God neither should nor can forgive me, but must confirm, praise, crown, and say: You have taught aright, for I have spoken through you and the Word is Mine. He who cannot boast thus of his sermon, let him leave preaching alone, for he surely lies and blasphemes God. . . . Life may well be sin and wrong, yea alas it is only too wrong: but **doctrine** must he absolutely straight and certain, without all sin. Therefore in the Church nothing but the certain, pure and only Word of God must be preached. When that is lacking then it is no longer the Church, but the devil's school." *(Against Hans Worst.)*

4. This still leaves us with a few, very few, churches which lay claim to teaching the full, uncorrupted, apostolic Faith. And it is certainly illogical to argue that since there are several conflicting claims to truth, therefore there is no truth! One might just as well reason as follows: The insane asylums of the world contain many people who claim to be Napoleon; therefore Napoleon never existed! The very existence of the counterfeit product in fact suggests that there is a real, genuine article! How can the sincere seeker decide among the conflicting claims, and select, from among the various denominations Christ's True Visible Church? Again, this is possible only if there are objective criteria or signposts, in other words, *marks of the Church.*

II. The True Marks of the Church: God's Word and Sacraments.
If genuine faith alone makes one a member of the Church, and if the Word and Sacraments of God alone are the means of grace whereby the

6

Holy Spirit creates and nourishes spiritual life, that is, faith, it follows that these outward, recognizable means of grace—and the Gospel always presupposes the Law—are the infallible marks which indicate the presence of the Church.

The Word of God is the seed, out of which grows the wheat, that is, the Church, the believers. Matt. 13:24 ff. The Gospel, then, creates the Church. In this world, however, the wheat and the tares grow together, and cannot be separated, vv. 25-29. The true wheat field cannot be known except by the seed, that is, God's Word, which is sown. And that seed is never sown in vain. Is. 55:10-11.

Since Christ founded His Church upon the Apostles and Prophets (Eph. 2:20), it follows that apostolic (that is, scriptural) doctrine is the mark of the Church, while the rejection of this doctrine is, to that extent, rebellion against Christ, and is therefore a mark of the counterfeit or anti-Church, with which, *as such*, the orthodox, faithful Church can needless to say—practice or cultivate no spiritual-fraternal relations of any kind whatever.

And the Sacraments, that is, Holy Baptism and Holy Communion, are but different forms of the same Gospel, and therefore are also not empty symbols and ceremonies, but powerful, life-giving, faith-creating means of grace: "Except a man be born of water and of the Spirit, he cannot enter into the Kingdom of God," John 3 : 5; "That He might sanctify and cleanse it (the Church) with the washing of water by the word," Eph. 5 : 26; "Drink ye all of it; for this is my blood of the new testament, which is shed for many *for the remission of sins*" Matt. 26 : 27, 28; "There are three that bear witness in earth, the Spirit, and the water, and the Wood: and these three agree in one," 1 John 5 : 8.

This is also the official teaching of the Lutheran Church in her Confessions:-

> The Church is not merely an association of outward ties and rites like other civic governments, however, but it is mainly an association of faith and of the Holy Spirit in men's hearts. To make it recognizable, this association has outward marks, the pure teaching of the Gospel and the administration of the sacraments in harmony with the Gospel of Christ. This Church alone is called the body of Christ, which Christ renews, consecrates, and governs by his Spirit. . . .
> We have not said anything new. Paul defined the Church in the same way in Eph. 5 ; 25-27, saying that it should he purified in order to be holy. He also added the outward marks, the Word and the Sacraments. . .
> We are not dreaming about some Platonic republic, as has been slanderously alleged, but we teach that this Church actually exists, made up of true believers and righteous men scattered throughout the world. And we add its marks, the pure teaching of the Gospel and the Sacraments. (*Apology of the Augsburg Confession*, VII VIM. 5.7.20.)

Dr. C. F. W. Walther, in his famous book The Evangelical Lutheran Church, the True Visible Church of God on Earth, puts it this way:—
> The one holy Christian Church, being a spiritual temple, can indeed

7

not be seen, but can only be believed; yet there are infallible external marks, by which her existence is known, which marks are the pure preaching of the Word of God and the unadulterated administration of the holy Sacraments (Thesis II).

And in his classic work on the Church and the Ministry, Dr. Walther gives the following interesting quotes from other great theologians:—

St Jerome:

The Church consists not in walls, but in the truth of her doctrines. The Church is where the true Faith is.

St. John Chrysostom:

When you see, in the holy place of the Church, a godless sect, which is an army of the Antichrist, then let him who is in Judea flee unto the mountains, that is, let him who is in Christendom turn to Holy Scripture. For the true Judea is Christendom, and the mountains are the writings of the prophets and apostles. But why does (the Lord) command that all Christians should at that time turn to Scripture? . . . Knowing full well that there will be such a great confusion in the last days, the Lord therefore commands the Christians, who are in Christendom and wish to attain firmness of faith, that they should find refuge in nothing else than Scripture. Otherwise, if they look to anything else, they will take offense and be lost, for they will not recognize which is the Church, and thereby fail into the abomination of desolation, which stands in the holy place of the Church.

St. Augustine:

If you seek Him who first sought you, and have become His sheep, and hear the voice of your Shepherd and follow Him, then heed what He shows you concerning Himself, and concerning His (spiritual) Body, lest you be mistaken about Him, lest you be mistaken about the Church; so that no one say to you, "It is Christ", when it is not Christ, or "It is the Church", when it is not the Church, etc. Hear the voice of the Shepherd Himself, He shows Himself to you, follow His voice; He also shows you the Church, that no one deceive you with the name of the Church.

Dr. Martin Luther:

But you might say: If now the Church is completely in the Spirit, and is a completely spiritual thing, then no one will be able to know where in the whole world there is a piece of her; that would be a strange, unheard of thing...Now you ask, by which sign must I then recognize the Church? Since there must be a sign given, whereby we are gathered together to hear the Word of God? Answer: Yes, such a sign is necessary, and we also have it: namely Baptism, the Bread, and above all the Gospel. These three are the Christians' slogan and badge. Where you see these in use, that is, Baptism, the Bread, and the Gospel, wherever or among whomever it may be, do not doubt, that the Church is there. For Christ willed that we all be agreed in these three signs, as St. Paul says in Eph. 4; 5: "One Lord, one Faith, one Baptism". Indeed, the Gospel is the one, the surest, and the noblest sign of the Church, much surer than Baptism and the Bread;

for she (the Church) is conceived, made, nourished, born, brought up, pastured, dressed, ornamented, strengthened, armed, and preserved alone by the Gospel.

And:

Thus all are called Christians, and all have the Gospel, but only one-fourth of the seed remains good and brings fruit. Such Christian people I have never yet seen on earth. . . . The persons I cannot number, but this I can say: where the Gospel is, there are Christians.

And:

For it is God's Word which creates the Church; that is the Lord over all places: in whichever place the same is heard, there you must regard it as quite certain, must conclude and say: Here certainly is God's House, here heaven is open.

Once it is pointed out that God's Word and Sacraments are the marks of the Church, it all seems very natural and obvious. Yet false teachers, in the interests of their false teachings and churches, have invented other "marks", by which they have tried to show that their particular organization was or is the true visible Church of God on earth. Some of these misleading, in fact, fraudulent "marks" can be made to look very convincing, and many people are in fact deceived by them. Let us therefore look at a number of these pretended "marks":—

1. Name: Cardinal Robert Bellarmine claimed that the name "catholic" (meaning: universal, general) was a necessary mark of the Church, and that the Roman Church was therefore the true Church. Actually, the mere name, by itself, means nothing. It merely sets up a claim which remains to be proved. *The Roman Church is not catholic, because she condemns the catholic Faith*, that is, the Faith which Christ and His Apostles have once and for all made binding for the whole, universal (catholic) Church. Similarly, the so-called Eastern Orthodox Church calls itself both catholic and orthodox; yet the mere name does not change the reality. The followers of Alexander Campbell call themselves the "Church of Christ", and think that therefore they are! Again we reply: Prove it, by showing that you have Christ's doctrine and Sacraments!

On the other hand, the fact that a denomination was called "Lutheran" by its enemies, and that this name has "stuck" through history, does not prove that the church so labelled is merely a sect which follows the private opinions of one man. This has happened before in the history of the Church. Thus, in the fourth century the Arian heretics called the true Church "Athanasians", because St. Athanasius was the chief defender of the true Scriptural doctrine that Christ is true God, which doctrine the Arians denied. Now, no matter how much the true, orthodox Church was maligned as being "Athanasian," it still represented the one, holy, catholic, and apostolic Church, because it confessed the one true Scriptural Faith.

It must also be understood very clearly that the mere fact that a body calls itself "Lutheran", does not mean that it really is Lutheran. Only those congregations and synods are really Lutheran which actually teach and administer the Sacraments according to the Scriptures, as laid down in the Lutheran Confessions. A church which calls itself Lutheran, but tolerates false (for example, Roman Catholic, Reformed, or modernistic) teachings, or practices church-fellowship with Reformed or other sects, is not really a Lutheran Church.

Let us take an example from modern church-life. The Lutheran World Federation is an organization which claims to be Lutheran because its constitution contains this "doctrinal basis" (Art. II): "The Lutheran World Federation acknowledges the Holy Scriptures of the Old and New Testaments as the only source and the infallible norm of all Church doctrine and practice, and sees in the Confessions of the Lutheran Church, especially in the Un-altered Augsburg Confession and Luther's Catechism, a pure exposition of the Word of God." So far so good. We would certainly have to agree that an organization which practiced these words would indeed be Lutheran. But then we discover that the L.W.F. welcomes as members churches which:—

(1)   are not Lutheran at all, but are parts of unionistic churches in which Reformed and Lutheran doctrine have, officially, the same rights and standing (the Church of Pomerania, for example);

(2)   are Lutheran in name, but permit all sorts of heresies, including denial of the very fundamentals of the Faith, such as the Divinity of Christ, the Redemption, the Inspiration of Scripture. We could name here practically all European Lutheran state churches, and "The Lutheran Church in America";

(3)   are officially in fellowship (inter-communion!) with Reformed and modernistic churches (the Church of Sweden, for example, is in fellowship with the Church of England).

When this sort of thing is pointed out to the leaders of the Lutheran World Federation, they reply that the Federation has no actual doctrine, but only a *doctrinal basis* (letter of the Secretary of the Executive Committee to President Stolz of the U.E.L.C.A. July 15th, 1953), and that the Federation cannot interfere in the internal affairs of member churches. This means that every member church is free to interpret the "doctrinal basis" as it likes, no matter how heretical that may be! The only principle which can be deduced from this practice is that, as far as the Federation is concerned, Lutheran doctrine is whatever anybody would like it to be or says it is, provided only that he remember to call it "Lutheran!"

In other words, the Federation, in calling itself Lutheran, is relying upon a mere formality, that is, upon the *name* of the Lutheran Confessions, not upon the actual content. Hence the Federation is Lutheran in name only, not in fact. Anybody which *really* "sees in the Confessions of the Lutheran Church . . . a pure exposition of the Word of God" cannot nonchalantly accept as Lutheran, churches and individuals who see in the Lutheran Confessions nothing of the kind!

But the Word and Sacraments are marks of the Church not in the sense that they are merely to be confessed officially in some constitution (paper is patient!), but in the sense that they are actually to be taught, practiced, and confessed. The "Word" means the actual doctrine or teaching of the Gospel, not a mere "basis", that is, a waxen nose, which anyone may twist as he pleases! *Actual* right teaching, and *actual* right administration of the Sacraments are meant. After all, even Rome accepts Scripture as a "doctrinal basis!" But what does she build upon that basis? That is the question.

No mere names, such as "catholic", "orthodox", "Christian", or "Lutheran," are decisive. Not the *names*, but the actual substance or *content* of Word (right doctrine!) and Sacraments are the marks of the Church. Acceptance of "Word and Sacraments" *in name only* is a meaningless formality, an empty gesture—and in matters involving the honor and the holy name of God, empty gestures are out of the question for anyone who still remembers the Second Commandment.

2. Age: N. Hunnius writes in his *Dogmatics:*—

> We must not be concerned about other marks of the Church, as for instance, its age; so that that Church is to be regarded as the right one which is the oldest. . . . At the time when Christ the Lord and His Apostles preached in Judea, His Church was regarded as new and the Pharisees and their followers as the old body; and yet Christ's Church was founded on the first sermon (Gen. 3, 5) and was therefore the oldest; whereas the assembly of the Pharisees was not older than their doctrine, which their elders had invented only some time before Christ's advent. When God willed to set apart a people to serve Him, from among the relationship of Abraham, and thereupon led him out of Chaldea, Abraham already had a church in his homeland, in which he together with his ancestors served other gods (Jos. 24 : 2). When Abraham now initiated a new Church, the idolatrous church in Chaldea was the older: consequently, if age were the determining factor, the church in Abraham's home would have to be regarded as a false church, and the idolatrous church of his forefathers as the true church. When the doctrine of Christ was carried into the world by the apostles, it was regarded as something new (Acts 17. 18); verse 19: "May we know what this new doctrine, whereof thou speakest is?" Over against this, idolatry was old. If, therefore, we were to judge with respect to age, idolatry would be right, the teaching of St. Paul wrong. (Nie. Hunnius *Dogmatik*, 405-406.)

And yet, how many souls are seduced by the deceptive argument from age! Fossils are old, too: but they are not alive, even though their shapes resemble those of living creatures! ,

3. Numbers: Luther somewhere described the main argument of his opponents thus: "There's many of us, and we wish to have it so. Therefore *we are right!" Yet the true Church has often been—in fact she probably always is—statistically a hopeless minority.* Who had the vast numbers and majorities on their side, Noah or his opponents? Elijah or the idolaters? Christ or the Pharisees? "Wide is the gate and broad is the way," says our Lord, "that leadeth to destruction, and many there be which go in there at: Because strait is the gate and narrow is the way, which leadeth unto life, and few there be that find it." Matt. 7: 14.

Numbers and majority votes, then, prove exactly nothing. Yet how many people are troubled, even deceived, by the argument: "So many mil-

11

lions can't be wrong"!

4. Prestige: The more unspiritual people are, the more they are impressed with the argument: "Look how many wise, great, noble, rich, and learned men are on our side!" Big, beautiful, rich churches, patronized by the high and mighty of this world, are the old Adam's ideal of true religion! And the old Adam must also have the wisdom of the world on his side. But what all does the holy Apostle say?

> Ye see your calling, brethren, how that *not many wise men after the flesh, not many mighty, not many noble, are called:* But God hath chosen the foolish things of the world to confound the wise . . . (I Cor. 1:18-31).

5. Unity or oneness: As Dr. Nickel, a former General President of our synod has pointed out in an essay on Church fellowship: "also the kingdom of Satan is united!"

The holy Christian Church indeed possesses perfect spiritual unity: "One Lord, one Faith, one Baptism." Eph. 4 : 5. But this unity, like the Church herself, can be grasped nowhere else but only in the marks, that is, in the pure Gospel and the Sacraments. External union, that is, the accommodation of conflicting teachings under one roof, is not the true unity of the Church, but a caricature of it (The devil, says Luther, is "God's ape"). This kind of outward union, despite inner conflicts of teachings, we find in Rome, and especially in the major Reformed sects of our day, as well as in much of nominal "Lutheranism".

6. Sanctity or holiness: To quote Dr. Nickel again: "as far as holiness is concerned, it is either an outward thing, which also hypocrites can make a show of, or it is an inward matter of the heart, and this we cannot see. So holiness cannot be a mark of the true visible church."

Again, the holiness of the Church, like the Church herself, is an article of Faith, not something which can be visibly demonstrated. And the holiness of the Church is above all not the imperfect holiness of its members (sanctification), but the perfect, imputed holiness of Christ (justification). The *Apology of the Augsburg Confession* warns:—

> False teachers should not be received or heard; for they no longer represent Christ, but are antichrists. . . . Aside from this, as regards the priests' own life, Christ has admonished us, in the parables of the Church, that we should not create schisms or divisions if the priests or the people do not everywhere lead pure, Christian lives as the Donatists did. (VII, 48-49.)

And Luther writes:

> Therefore we confess correctly in the Creed when we say: "We *believe* one holy Christian Church"; for she is *invisible*, and lives in the Spirit, at a place to which no one can come; wherefore her holiness cannot be seen. For God so covers and hides her with weakness, sins, errors, with various afflictions and offenses that we can nowhere find her with our senses. People who do not know this, and see how those who have been baptized and have and believe the Gospel, still have weakness, sin and other shortcomings, immediately take offense, and hold that such do not belong to the Church; then they get the

12

idea that the true Church are only the unspiritual ones, that is, the Pope with his throng, because they outwardly behave differently, with respect to clothing, food, places, etc ., than the common Christian (which human reason regards much and highly) .... Those who have such ideas about the Church, completely reverse that article of our Creed in which we say: "*I believe* one holy Christian Church," and turn believing into seeing (*Galatians*).

Such fanatical sects as the Pentecostals of our day, also make a great to-do about their supposed piety, zeal, and spirituality, and attack the orthodox Church for her supposed coldness and indifference. Actually, true Christian devotion is humble, quiet, unostentatious, and unassuming (Matt. 6: 1-18). Therefore it is easily outshone by the glitter of a false, Pharisaic, "camera-conscious" and therefore counterfeit "piety." Let no man judge by appearances! The whole idea that we must look for the Church by looking for great apparent holiness among her members, is the devil's trick to lead men away from the outward marks, that is, the Gospel and the Sacraments, and into the quicksands of human subjectivism and fanaticism. *Faith must rest in God and His Word, not in men and their holiness or lack of it!* Besides, false teachers are especially careful to disguise themselves in the "sheep's clothing" (Matt. 7 : 15) of an outwardly pious and zealous life. The disguise is very effective, as the following warped judgment by a modern author proves:—

Many heretics, whose opinions the Church had to condemn, were men of saintly character, actuated only by the sincerest desire to promote the true religion of the Lord Jesus. For example, Appolinarius in the fourth century was a saintly and Christ-like scholar and bishop, beloved even by those who had to condemn his view . . . it is true to say that on the whole the greatest heretics—the "heresiarchs"—were honest Christians, zealous for the promotion of a true and reverent Christian theology. (Alan Richardson, *Creeds in the Making,* p. 33.)

Neither is apparent outward holiness a mark of the Church, nor is the absence of it a sign that the Church is absent. Dr. Nickel writes, in the work quoted before:—

A holy, pious life is not the mark of the orthodox church. This was the error of the Donatists, a sect which had its origin in the fourth century, and which taught that that church was a true church which had no unbelievers and hypocrites among its members. Against this Christ tells us in His Word, namely in the parables, that just as in the heap of fishes the good and the bad lie intermingled, so the Church is hidden here among the great multitude of the godless. And how deplorable were conditions in the congregation at Corinth. Grave deficiencies existed there as far as Christian life was concerned. A member of that congregation had married his stepmother, and led an incestuous life with her. And the congregation had done nothing to remove this great offense. What now did the Apostle Paul do? Did he say to the members: You faithful and upright ones, leave this congregation; it practices no church discipline, therefore it is no

13

orthodox congregation?

Nothing of the kind. On the contrary he calls them the Church of God, sanctified in Christ Jesus, the called saints. But this he says to them: "Let there be no divisions among you, but be ye perfectly joined together in the same mind and in the same judgment" (I Cor. 1:2.10). Consequently, conditions in a congregation with respect to church discipline may be ever so deplorable, and of such a nature that it cannot even be considered feasible to discipline manifest sinners and excommunicate them according to the instructions of the Apostle, yet a Christian has neither the duty nor the right to say: Now I am going to leave this congregation, for here there is no longer any obedience to the dear Word of the Lord and the clear instruction of the Apostle; for as long as the congregation still has the character of orthodoxy, one must remain with it and testify.

This, by the way, does not mean that Christians may remain in fellowship with bodies which do not practice doctrinal discipline, but allow false teachers openly to spread their errors. For then the very marks of the Church themselves, the pure doctrine of the Gospel and the Sacraments, would be attacked. Such a church is no longer orthodox.

It should also be stated that there is a limitation on the extent to which the absence of discipline in life and morals must be tolerated. If it is apparent that a congregation is not merely weak or lax in the application of God's Word, but in principle despises that Word, and has no intention of applying it, then this automatically becomes a *doctrinal* issue, and must be treated accordingly.

*Throughout Christian Church history, unionists and church-politicians have always appealed to **love,** when false doctrine was being attacked.* Let Martin Luther, in his own inimitable way, explode this unspiritual notion:—

We are indeed ready and willing to have peace with them and show them love; yet only insofar as they leave us the doctrine of faith unharmed and unfalsified. If we cannot obtain this from them, it is useless that they praise Christian love so highly. Cursed into the depths of hell be the love which is maintained at the expense of harm and detriment to the doctrine of faith, before which absolutely everything must give way, be it love, apostle, angel from heaven, or whatever else it may be. . . . Because they regard this matter of such small and insignificant consequence, they thereby give us very plainly to understand just how they regard the majesty and glory of the Divine Word. If they earnestly and in their hearts believed that it is really the Word of God, they would not thus trifle and play with it, but hold it in the highest esteem. . . . Therefore we let them praise Christian love as much as they like. We, on the contrary, laud and praise the majesty and glory of the Word and of faith. Love can be somewhat diminished without incurring harm and danger; but this cannot happen with the Word and faith. Love should suffer everything and give way before everybody; but faith cannot and must not suffer anything; in short, it cannot and must not give way before anybody. . ."He that

14

troubleth you shall bear his judgment, whosoever he be." (Gal 5:10.) With these words St. Paul condemns the false apostles so powerfully", as though he pronounced sentence upon them from the judgment seat of Christ, and calls them by a very nasty name, "The Confusers of the Galatians," for the good Galatians regarded them as exceptionally holy men and far better teachers than St. Paul himself. We may well assume from the words "whosoever he be", that the false apostles according to their outward appearance were very pious and holy people; it could even be that among them there was a man of outstanding reputation, a disciple of the true apostles themselves, who commanded great respect and enjoyed much popularity; St. Paul certainly does not without reason use such mighty and powerful words. Also it cannot be doubted that many of them were greatly offended at these violent words of the Apostle, and thought thus: Why does St. Paul so quickly dispense with love? Why is he so stubborn and self-willed in such a small and inconsequential matter? Why does he so soon hand over to the devil and eternal perdition those who are as much servants of Christ as he is?

All such things do not concern him in the least, but since they falsify the doctrine of faith, he curses and condemns them in no uncertain terms; moreover, he has not the slightest doubt, but that he is doing the right thing to them, and says boldly: "Those who confuse you will bear their judgment".

Therefore we must, as I have pointed out again and again, diligently distinguish between doctrine and life. Doctrine is heaven, life is the earth. In life there is sin, error, disunity, nothing but trouble and labor. There love is to close its ears and overlook things—*But with doctrine it is an altogether different matter*; for doctrine is holy, clean, pure, heavenly, divine. Whoever wants to alter this or falsify it, towards him neither love nor mercy is to be shown, and such action needs no forgiveness of sin. . . . *Our doctrine is, by God's grace, pure.* There is not one single article of our faith for which we have not a good, solid, scriptural foundation. These the devil would love to besmirch and pervert. Therefore he attacks us so insidiously with this argument which he hurls at us through the rabble, that we are responsible for everything, that we do not keep peace, that we are quarrelsome, that we disrupt unity and love in the Church or in Christendom. Therefore we should learn to regard most highly the majesty and glory of the Word: for it is not such a small and trifling thing as the fanatics of our time hold it to be, for one single i-dot is greater and far more important than heaven and earth. Therefore we in this matter show no concern whatever for Christian unity or love, but at once use the judgment-seat, that is, we curse and condemn all those who in the least little point falsify or injure the majesty of the Word, for "a little leaven leaveneth the whole lump." *(Commentary on Galatians.)*

As the First Table of the Law comes before the Second, so love for God. His Word, and His Church, must come before all other loves. Matt. 10:37.

15

The playwright Ibsen puts these words into the mouth of Pastor Brand: "What the world calls love I neither know or want. I know God's love, and that is not weak and gentle, but hard: its caresses leaves wounds!" Yes, true. Biblical, redemptive love is always dominated from above, by the keen edge of the First Commandment. It throbs with the crimson of fire and of blood—it does not ooze with the timid and disgusting pinks of mere sentimentality and "humanitarianism." "Charity," writes the Apostle St. Paul, "rejoiceth not in iniquity, but rejoiceth in the truth," I Cor. 13:6. Unionism, on the other hand, is doctrinally flabby and spineless and therefore, far from rejoicing in the truth dreads and condemns it as bigotry, pride, stubbornness, fanaticism, intolerance, and the like. We can be very sure therefore that any course of action whose total effect is the protection of error and errorists, and the suppression of those who protest against the error, is the very opposite of Christian love, even though it disguises itself in the garments of the latter! And Church history teaches us to suspect-that he who builds his case on a plea for love, is trying to avoid the issue! Here Luther must be our guide: "Accursed be that charity . . . !"

7. Miracles: Both Rome and the Pentecostals put heavy emphasis on miracles, as proving the truth of their respective churches. Now, exactly the same sort of "miracles," particularly healings, are claimed for such widely divergent denominations as Roman Catholicism, Pentecostalism, and Christian Science, for example. We might add also such pagan religions affirms what the others deny, the "miracles" themselves cannot be taken as proof of the truth of their respective doctrines. The same logic which the Pentecostal uses to show that his is the true church, can be used by Rome to "prove" the truth of Mary-worship (Lourdes), or by Christian Science to "disprove" the doctrine of the Trinity!

This is not the place to explain these conflicting "miracles". Suffice it to say that aside from ordinary fraud there are three possibilities: In the first place, a large number of "healings" and other "miraculous" manifestations ("tongues") may be due to perfectly natural causes, which the relatively new science of parapsychology is now beginning to study. Who knows what abilities and instinctive powers, once given to mankind in Creation, have survived the Fall, in one form or another, as sin-ridden remnants? S.A. Hill, in his pamphlet, "Modern New Tongues," discusses Pentecostal "healings" and "tongues," and shows that they may be as natural as ordinary hypnotism! In the second place, especially when the "miracle" directly supports some false doctrine, the work of Satan must be suspected: "...after the working of Satan with all power and signs and lying wonders," 2 Thes. 2:9. And of course Satan can also make use of otherwise perfectly natural forces and laws and even of sincere and Christian persons (Matt. 16:23). In the third place, finally, God in his providence, may have his good reasons for granting true miracles also outside the Church of the pure Word and Sacraments, just as there is spiritual life even in heretical sects, so long as enough of the substance of the Gospel is still there to create saving faith. Naturally God never grants miracles in confirmation of false doctrine. The great Church Father St.

16

Augustine (353-430), thus refutes a false church's (the Donatists') appeal to miracles:—

> Prove to me your church, but not by saying: It is true, because I say so, or because my colleague, or these bishops or clerics or our laymen say so; or it is true because this one or that one worked wonders, Donatus or Pontius, or whoever; or because men pray at the burial places of our dead and are heard, or because this or that happens there; or because this our brother or that our sister, waking, saw such vision, or dreaming dreamt such a vision. Away with these inventions of lying men or trick-flares of deceiving spirits! For either it is not true what is said there, or, if it is true, then we must beware of it so much the more; since the Lord also prophesied that there would be no lack of such as do signs and wonders, in order that, if it were possible, even the elect should be misled. Furthermore, if one who prays at the graves of heretics is heard, he is not heard on account of the merit of the place, but on account of the merit of his desire he receives either good or evil. For the Spirit of God, it is written, filleth the world. And many are heard, to whom God is opposed, according to the word of the Apostle: he gave them up to the lusts of their own hearts; while on the other hand God in His grace does not grant to many what they wish, in order to give them what is good for them. As for vision, we know that Satan too disguises himself as an angel of light, and that many have already been deceived by their dreams. One should only hear what sort of wondrous deeds and visions and heathen tell of their temples and gods. Many therefore are heard, and in different ways, not only catholic Christians, but also heathen, Jew, and heretics; but they are heard either by deceiving spirits, which cannot do anything except as they have permission from God, who in an exalted and inexpressible manner prepares for everyone what is his due, or (they are heard) by God Himself, either as a punishment of their wickedness, or as a comfort in their misery, or as an admonition to seek eternal salvation. Eternal salvation itself and eternal life no one can reach, except he who has Christ as his Head.

His own Church, argues St. Augustine, is the true one: —

> Not because Ambrose of Milan (is) in her, not because she is proclaimed to be such by the councils of our Church, or because in her, in holy places, there occur great miracles of answered prayer or of healings...Whatever of this sort happens in the catholic Church, is to be approved because it happens in the catholic Church; but the catholic Church is not proved to be such because such things happen within her. *The Law, the Prophets, and the Gospels, and their statements—that is the real testimony. All else is the smoke of earthly trick-flares compared to this thunder and lightning from above.* (Quoted in Boehringer, Kirchengesschichte, 1/3, pp. 320-321.)

8. "Apostolic Succession": The basic theory, as maintained with slight modifications by Roman Catholicism, Eastern Orthodox, and the Church of England, is as follows: The Apostles consecrated bishops, and

17

these bishops in turn consecrated other bishops, and so on, until the present day. Now only bishops which stand in this "lawful" succession, can properly ordain men into the Christian ministry. The Sacraments administered by men not so ordained are not valid. A church whose clergy lack this "apostolic succession," cannot be true and apostolic.

Scripture, of course, knows of no "apostolic succession" except a continuation in apostolic doctrine ("and they continued steadfastly in the *apostles' doctrine* and fellowship, and in breaking of bread, and in prayers," Acts 2 : 42). It is the Word which creates and rules the Church, and not the Church the Word. Therefore the Lutheran Church, in her *Tractate of the Power and Primacy of the Pope,* confesses:—

> When the regular bishops become enemies of the Gospel and are unwilling to administer ordination, the churches retain the right to ordain for themselves. For wherever the Church exists, the right to administer the Gospel also exists. Wherefore it is necessary for the Church to retain the right of calling, electing, and ordaining ministers. . . . Where the true Church is, therefore, the right of electing and ordaining ministers must of necessity also be (66-67).

And the Church Father Tertullian (d. 218 A.D.) writes:—

> They are true churches which hold fast what they have received from the Apostles, and the Apostles from Christ and Christ from God; other churches, which were not founded by the Apostles, are nevertheless if they are agreed in the same faith, to be regarded as no less apostolic, *on account of the kinship of doctrine.* (Quoted in Walther, *Kirche und Amt,* p. 61.)

It is interesting to note that several Lutheran churches of northern Europe (the Church of Sweden, for example) also have inherited the so-called "apostolic succession", that is, the unbroken line of bishops from apostolic times to the present. Unlike the Church of England, these Lutheran churches, we are told, do not make a *doctrinal* issue, or a necessity, of this "apostolic succession", but regard it as a helpful piece of tradition. Yet this "apostolic succession" has not saved these churches from serious doctrinal decay and corruption, as it has not saved Romanism, Eastern Orthodoxy, and Anglicanism from a similar fate. Any "succession" in mere externals, without the pure Gospel, is not apostolic, but apostatic. A fossil of a fish is simply not a fish! As the idolatrous priests and prophets of Israel's history, and the Pharisees and Sadducees of Christ's day, were not the true Church, but a heretical sect, despite their outward "succession" from Abraham and Moses, so the outward "successors" of the Apostles are not the true Church today, if they reject Apostolic doctrine, 1 John 2 : 1 9 ("They went out from us, but they were not of us"). "They have not the inheritance of Peter, who have not the faith of Peter," writes St. Ambrose (d. 397 A.D.). The succession depends on the Gospel, not the Gospel on the succession. It is the latter that must be judged by the former, not *vice versa.*

The same arguments hold true for any sort of external landmarks beyond and apart from Word and Sacraments. One high-church Anglican publication (*A Chart of Church History*) actually, in all seriousness, lists as one of five "essential elements of the Church":—

"WORSHIP: Vestments, altar, form of prayers." On these and similar grounds, the Lutheran Church and others are simply written off as sects, separate from the living stream of the Church, while the Church of England, together with Eastern Orthodoxy (a rather reluctant partner, on account of the Church of England's liberalism!), is presented as *the* true and historic Christian Church! A more dishonest, palpably false, and externalistic view of the Church it is difficult to imagine. In the first place, the Lutheran Church in fact does retain "vestments, altar, form of prayer," etc. In the second place, even if she used other forms, what of it, if Word and Sacrament are still there? The Church of England, on the other hand, permits almost every variety of doctrine and heresy, including Freemasonry, to flourish openly in her midst. Yet, even though she does not insist on such fundamentals as, say, the doctrine of the Trinity, this church claims to be Christian because she does insist on "vestments, altar, form of prayers," and other similar purely externalistic landmarks, especially, of course, the "apostolic succession"!

The Lutheran Church, in her Confessions, again and again calls men away from all forms of fanaticism, externalism, and traditionalism, back to true apostolicity, to the pure marks of the Church:—

> For it is sufficient for the true unity of the Christian Church that the Gospel be preached in conformity with a pure understanding of it and that the Sacraments be administered in accordance with the divine Word. It is not necessary for the true unity of the Christian Church that ceremonies, instituted by men, should be observed uniformly in all places. (*Augsburg Confession,* Art. VII.)

And:

> Churches will not condemn each other because of a difference in ceremonies, when in Christian liberty one uses fewer or more of them, as long as they are otherwise agreed in doctrine and in all its articles and are also agreed concerning the right use of the holy Sacraments, according to the well-known axiom, "Disagreement in fasting should not destroy agreement in faith". (*Formula of Concord*, Solid Declaration, Art. X, 31.)

III. The Right Use of the Marks of the Church.

We use the marks of the Church properly, when we let them determine and regulate our whole religious life, so that we worship no other God, know of no other Christ, and recognizes no other Spirit, except the God, Father, Son, and Holy Spirit, Who gives Himself in the Gospel, that is, in Word and Sacrament. Apart from these there are only imaginary gods, false "Christs," and evil spirits.

There are those who think that because true Christians are found wherever there is enough of the Gospel to create and sustain saving faith, even in heretical sects, therefore it does not make any difference to which "denomination" one belongs. Especially nowadays, on account of the doctrinal confusion in Christendom, people find it very hard to see that it matters to which "denomination" one belongs. Yet the fact remains that God commands His Christians to distinguish sharply between orthodox

19

(right teaching) and heterodox (differently-teaching) congregations and bodies, to belong only to the former, and in case they have strayed into heterodox bodies, to leave them:—

"Beware of false prophets, which come to you in sheep's clothing, but inwardly they are ravening wolves!" (Matt. 7:15.)

"Whosoever therefore shall confess Me before men, him will I confess also before My Father which is in heaven. But whosoever shall deny Me before men, him will I also deny before My Father which is in heaven." (Matt. 10:32-33.)

"teaching them to observe *all things* whatsoever I have commanded you." (Matt. 28 : 20.)

"Mark them which cause divisions and offenses contrary to the doctrine which you have learnt, and avoid them." (Rom. 16:17.)

"If any man preach any other gospel unto you than that ye have received let him be accursed." (Gal. 1:9.)

"A little leaven leaveneth the whole lump." (Gal. 5:9.)

"A man that is an heretic after the first and second admonition reject." (Tit. 3:10.)

"We have an altar whereof they have no right to eat which serve the tabernacle." (Hebrews 13:10.)

"If there come any unto you and bring not this doctrine, receive him not into your house, neither bid him God speed: for he that biddeth him God speed is partaker of his evil deeds." (2 John 10:11.)

And not only are Christians to belong only to orthodox congregations and church-bodies, but they are also to avoid any sort of spiritual, religious fellowship with heterodox, or false churches, and that for the same reasons.

This position has always been held and practised by the orthodox Church:

In his book on the practice of church-fellowship in the ancient Church, Prof. Werner Elert, a European Lutheran theologian, makes the following statements:—

There is either complete fellowship, or none at all. (***Abendmahl und Kirchengemeinschaft in der alien Kirche,*** p. 136.)

According to the report of Epiphanius, the schism between Bishop Meletius of Lycopolis and Peter of Alexandria came to a head in this that "the one party and the other prayed separately, and likewise each performed the other holy ministrations for himself", that is, by suspending prayer and sacramental fellowship. (p. 138.)

Church fellowship is as indivisible as the Church herself, this was recognized by all alike. (p. 142.)

"The Evangelical Lutheran Church," writes Dr. C.F.W. Walther, "rejects all brotherly and churchly fellowship with those who reject her confession, be it wholly or in part" (our dark-type emphasis). (***The Evangelical Lutheran Church, the True Visible Church of God on Earth***, Thesis XXIC.)

And the Lutheran Church as a whole confesses:

It is difficult to separate from so many countries and people, and to

20

maintain a different doctrine. But here we have God's command, that everyone should beware of and not be associated with such as maintain false doctrine or seek to preserve it by means of cruelty. (*Tractate of the Power and Primacy of the Pope*, 42.)

Dr. George Major received the following famous words of warning from Dr. Martin Luther:—

He who regards his doctrine, faith, and confession as true, correct, and certain, cannot stand in the same stable with others who represent false doctrine, or are given to it. . . . A teacher who is silent about the errors, and nevertheless wants to be a true teacher, is worse than an open fanatic, and with his hypocrisy does greater damage than a heretic, and he is not to be trusted; he is a wolf and a fox, a hireling and a belly-server, etc., and dares to despise and betray doctrine. Word, faith, Sacrament, churches and schools; he is either secretly lying under one blanket with the enemies, or he is a doubter and weather-vane and wants to see how things are going to go, whether Christ or the devil will prevail, or else he is quite uncertain in his own mind, and is not worthy to be called a student, much less a teacher, and does not wish to anger anyone, neither speak Christ's Word, nor hurt the devil and the world.

Luther also writes:—

"A little leaven leaveneth the whole lump." Just as in philosophy, if one errs a little in the beginning (in first principles), a very great and disproportionate error comes of it in the end, so also it goes in Theology, that a small error can spoil and falsify the entire Christian doctrine. Therefore doctrine and life must be thoroughly distinguished from one another. Doctrine isn't ours, but God's, Who has called us only as servants and ministers to it: therefore we neither must nor can yield or surrender the very smallest dot or letter of it. . . .

If they earnestly and from the heart believed that it is God's Word, they would not jest and play with it so frivolously, but hold it in the highest esteem, and without all doubt and disputation believe what it tells them: they would also know that one Word of God is all, and all Words of God are one; they would know that all the articles of our Christian Faith are one, and again, that one is all, and where one lets go of one, the others will certainly also collapse, in time: for they all hang together and belong together. (Galatians Commentary.)

Altogether too often one comes across this point of view: "Yes, I know that church is wrong, but it is still possible to be saved there. So why worry?"

It is quite true that sincere Christians, dear children of God, even though they, out of simplicity and ignorance, belong to a false church, will be forgiven and saved. It is quite another matter when others, who know better, join false churches. Our great theologians of the past have called attention, in this connection, to Absalom's rebellion against his father, King David. Now, the mere fact that "two hundred men out of Jerusalem"

21

joined the rebellion "in their simplicity, and they knew not anything" (2 Sam. 15 : 11), did not give others the right to do likewise! And one cannot *deliberately* be ignorant, simple, or weak—against better knowledge! The Christian never asks "How close can I come to hell without falling in?" but: "How can I please Christ, my Lord and Savior?" The Christian is anxious to please and serve God, not to scheme and calculate how much he can possibly "get away with" and still be saved! He who does not give two pence for the will of Christ, but is concerned only about saving his selfish soul with the least possible amount of inconvenience, is an unregenerate, carnal scoffer and unbeliever. "Be not deceived, God is not mocked," warns Scripture, Gal. 6:7. Whoever wishes merely to sneak past hell, will certainly drop in and burn eternally!

"Whatsoever is not of faith," warns the Apostle St. Paul, Rom. 14:23, *"is sin!"* Especially is this true of all ecclesiastical action. Church-fellowship and its exercise are vital aspects of our life in God and hence require an absolutely certain and objective, not an uncertain and subjective foundation. Since faith finds certainty only in God's Word, it follows that it can only regard this Word and the Sacraments, in short, the marks of the Church, as a basis for any exercise of Church-fellowship. Our guesses as to who might be a Christian, our conjectures as to whom we might meet in heaven, *cannot* provide such a basis. The attempt is rank subjectivism and fanaticism. We cannot look into other people's hearts, but we can determine whether what they teach agrees with the divine truth of Scripture. It is therefore only on the latter, and never on the former, that the exercise of Church-fellowship must be based.

And in deciding whether a church is orthodox, it is not enough to see whether this pastor or that congregation teaches rightly, but it is necessary to see how the church *as a whole* stands, and with what other churches it is in religious fellowship. If the body as a whole is unionistic, that is, if in practice it gives truth and error equal rights, so that both orthodox and heterodox pastors can teach their doctrines undisturbed, or if the body is in fellowship with churches which represent or tolerate false doctrine, then the whole body must be shunned and avoided. That is what it means to judge not by appearances, names, or personal likes or dislikes, but by the marks of the Church, the pure doctrine, and the properly administered Sacraments. Faithfulness and rebellion simply do not mix!

All this is expected, in principle, of those who become members of our congregations. For the form for "The Reception of New Members" printed in the *Church Liturgy for Evangelical Lutheran Churches in Australia* (p. 188) prescribes also this question (to be answered " I do"): "Do you purpose diligently to attend the preaching of the Divine Word and to partake of the blessed Sacrament of the Altar, and to *avoid participation in heterodox worship?*"

There are, however, some dangers in this connection which should be mentioned. It is quite possible to be very strict about doctrine and Church membership, but for entirely the wrong reason. It is possible to be staunchly orthodox merely out of stubbornness and pride, rather than out of sincere Christian faith! Dr. Walther, in a sermon on the Gospel for *In-*

vocavit, the first Sunday in Lent (Matt. 4 : 1-11), says:—

There are people who never experience trials on account of their faith. They therefore usually imagine themselves to have a really firm faith. Hence they also often say: No one is going to get me to abandon my faith; what I was born and baptized in, what my parents and teachers have taught me, and what I have sworn at my Confirmation, that's what I am going to remain with. Thus speak often just those who, with this their faith, live in various sins, in drunkenness, in greed, in misuse of God's Name, and the like.

Far from it, however, that when men never experience trials on account of their faith, this should be a sign of how firm a faith they have, this rather reveals that they are completely lacking in true faith. They are as yet spiritually dead, and therefore they never experience anything of those dangers which the spiritual life of a true Christian has. They experience nothing of the trials inflicted by the world, because they themselves still belong to the world. They experience nothing of the trials inflicted by Satan, because they are still captive to his will. They experience nothing of the trials inflicted by their reason, because their faith is nothing but a work of their reason. . . . They can preserve their own faith, they require for this purpose no diligent praying, no earnest watching, and no continual searching in God's Word, because they have made their faith themselves. No matter how many winds of temptation may blow, the light of their faith does not go out, because their faith is no real light in the heart, but only a manufactured light, an empty picture of their imagination. With true faith, however, it is an altogether different matter. True faith is a divine conviction of the truth of Holy Scripture and a divine confidence, that through Christ one is reconciled with God, is in a state of grace before God, is righteous before God, and an heir of eternal life. Such true faith no human being can give himself. It is created only by the Holy Spirit, in humbled, broken, and smashed hearts. And once a man has come into such a firm true faith, it costs watching and praying, to remain in this faith.

True faith looks only to the Gospel, by which it is created, and in which it lives. Therefore it looks to nothing but Word and Sacrament, when thinking about the Church. True, our parents, pastors, and teachers taught us beliefs and convictions long before we could even read. But *there comes a time when we ourselves must assume responsibility for what we believe.* It is not enough to believe something because one's parents believed it, or because such and such respected pastors and teachers have said so. That is not Christian faith at all. People who are Lutherans *by conviction*, rather than by lazy habit or tradition, believe that their Church is the true visible Church of God on earth, not because she makes that claim, not because Luther said so, nor because this or that person thinks so, but because this Church teaches God's Word correctly, and administers the holy Sacraments according to their institution by Christ, in short, because *she has the pure marks of Christ's Church.* To be guided by other considerations is not Christian. *True faith obeys Christ not Martin*

Luther.

Church-membership is a solemn and sacred matter, to be treated with fear and trembling. It is therefore horrible to hear expressions like "he turned for her", meaning: her husband, not being a Lutheran, joined the Lutheran Church after marriage. The Church cannot allow anyone to become a member for the sake of convenience or peace in the family. The only proper reason for joining the Church is for God's sake—not for the sake of anyone else, Matt. 10: 34-38. It must be a matter of personal conviction, and conscience; otherwise it is mockery. That is why the Lutheran Church does not receive anyone except upon proper and detailed instruction in the teachings of God's Word, which is the only basis upon which the individual can arrive at a responsible and God-pleasing decision. To join for the sake of one's husband, wife, or family, or for such personal reasons as that one likes the pastor, or finds the congregation friendly or congenial is no better than to join a church because of its better parking facilities (as an American journal reported it happens nowadays), or because its preacher tells more and better jokes (as has also happened in sectarian circles)!

A true Christian, whose church-membership is a matter of conviction, based on the Church's marks, not a matter of convenience, will then not regard and treat his congregation as some sort of a mere club, which one may join or leave at will. Rather, he will—by faith—see in his congregation the Family of God in that place, even though that Family be hidden under imperfections, offenses, and sins. The true Christian respects, fears, and honors above all earthly authority, that heavenly dignity with which Christ has invested His congregations on earth: "If he neglect to hear the Church, let him be unto thee as a heathen man and a publican. Verily I say unto you. Whatsoever ye shall bind on earth shall be bound in heaven: and whatsoever ye shall loose on earth shall be loosed in heaven," Matt. 18:17-18. The true Lutheran knows that his local congregation, even though small numerically, when compared with sectarian congregations, is nevertheless Christ's true visible Church in that place, which represents the one Universal Church, the Body of Christ. Thus the Lutheran never sees his Church as merely one sect among others, but as *the* Church which—by virtue of the *marks*—represents the Faith of the entire invisible Church of Christ and therefore of *all* Christians, to the extent that they are Christians. A true Lutheran is only one who believes that his Church represents the one Lord and the one Faith, into which all Christians are baptized in the one Baptism, Eph. 4 : 5 . A person, on the other hand, who leaves his congregation and Church as soon as he gets into embarrassing or annoying situations—perhaps the pastor, an elder, or a fellow member steps on his toes, rightly or wrongly—shows thereby that he has no idea of what the Church is, or else that he despises her and her Lord thoroughly! The Christian knows that the Church must please Christ, not men. A faith founded on Word and Sacrament, will cling to the Church so tenaciously that it will suffer all, even death, rather than fall away from her! May God grant such a faith to us all!

Finally, although Almighty God does command His children to seek

24

Him only where He may be found, namely in His Word and Sacraments, and although He commands them to observe all things whatsoever He has commanded, and to beware of and avoid all false teachings, teachers, and churches, nevertheless we are forbidden to do this in a proud, haughty, self-satisfied, Pharisaic manner, Gal. 6:1. Orthodox Christians, while they must be certain of the truth, must never be carnally secure in it, as if their faith and orthodoxy were not a gift of the Spirit, but their own achievement. And they must not hate and despise other Christians who are less fortunate. Even while we "hate every false way" (Ps. 119 : 104), even though we must uncompromisingly defend truth and attack error, even though we must on occasion be stern and hard—privately perhaps in anguish and tears, like Joseph with his brethren—we must never forget ardently to love Christ's whole Church on earth, and to pray especially for those poor souls who languish under the spiritual tyranny of error and false doctrine. Blind, stupid hatred and fanaticism are un-Christian. We hate and oppose falsehood and false religion, and the organizations which represent them, precisely because we love the dear children of God, our brethren in Christ, who are the victims of these various systems. We would not help these Christians, nor advance the unity of the Church, but, on the contrary, attack it, if we would acknowledge as legitimate their spiritual oppressors by practicing any form of Church-fellowship with them. Only if we restrict such Church-fellowship, and exercise it solely on the basis of the Church's marks, are we truly serving Christ, His one Church, and all Christians everywhere. Luther teaches us the right attitude, when he writes:—

We must confess that the fanatics have Scripture and God's Word in other articles, and whoever hears and believes it from them will be saved, even though they are unholy heretics and blasphemers of Christ. . . I say that under the Pope there exists true Christendom, yea the very select company of Christendom and many pious and great Saints. . . Hear for yourself what St. Paul says, 2 Thess. 2:4: The Antichrist will sit in the *temple of God*. If now the Pope is, as I firmly believe the true Antichrist, then he must "sit" or reign not in the Devil's stable, but in the "temple of God". No, he is not going to sit where there are only devils and unbelievers or where there is no Christ or Christendom; for he is supposed to be an Antichrist, and must therefore be among Christians. And because he must sit and reign there, he must have Christians under him. For "the temple of God "means not a pile of stones, but holy Christendom, 1 Cor. 3:17, in which he is to reign. . . . Therefore we do not rave like the fanatics, who condemn everything which the Pope has under him; for thus we would condemn also Christendom, the temple of God, with everything she has from Christ. But this is what we attack: That the Pope is not satisfied with these treasures of Christendom, which he has inherited from the Apostles, but adds his devil's addition over and above that, and uses these treasures not for the improvement of the temple of God but for its destruction, so that his commandments and order are held higher than Christ's order; although in this destruction Christ nevertheless preserves His Christendom. . . .Therefore that talk of the Anabaptists and fanatics amounts to nothing when they say: What the Pope has is wrong, or, because this or that is done in the Papacy, therefore we want to have it differently. Just as if they wanted to prove thereby that they are great enemies of the anti-Christ, but don't see that they greatly strengthen him thereby, greatly weaken Christendom, and deceive themselves. The abuse and the addition they should help us reject; but in that they wouldn't have much honor because they see that they couldn't be the first ones in that. Therefore they attack what no one else has yet attacked, in order that they might also be "first", and gain a bit of honor. But the honor must be turned into shame: for they attack the temple of God, and miss the Antichrist who sits in it; like blind people who reach for water and get into fire. Yes, they do as one brother did to the other in the Thuringian Forest: They are walking through the Forest together, when a bear attacks them, and grabs one of them and holds him under. The other one wants to help his brother, stabs after the bear, but misses him, and tragically stabs the brother under the bear. The fanatics do the same thing: they should help poor Christendom which the Antichrist has under himself and which he tortures, and so they set themselves ferociously against the Pope, but miss him, and far more tragically murder Christendom under the Pope. For if they would leave Baptism and the Sacrament intact, the Christians under the Pope could still escape with their souls and be saved, as happened hitherto; but now if the Sacraments are taken from them, they must be lost, for Christ Himself is taken away thereby. My dear, that's not the way to come bursting upon the Pope, because Christ's Saints lie under him. It takes a cautious, modest spirit, which would let remain under him that which is the temple of God, and resist the addition, with which he destroys the temple of God. (*Of Re-baptizing,* 1528 A.D.)

Pray for the Church, dear brethren, as never before! The times are evil, the perils great. Pray especially for the Church's seminaries, and for her public teachers and officials that God may grant them true steadfastness and courage, faith and wisdom! And let no devil, masquerading as an angel of light, lead you away from the Church's true marks, the divine Word and Sacraments. To go by these marks, and to refuse to be guided by any other considerations, no matter how near and dear they may appear, simply means walking by **faith**, rather than by **sight**. A Church **seen** rather than believed is to that extent a false church! The one true Church, which faith grasps only in her marks, is the Body of Christ Himself. "And blessed is he, whosoever shall not be offended in Me!" (Matt. 11:6.) Lord, we believe, help Thou our unbelief! Arise, plead Thine own cause! Let not man prevail! Save Thy people and bless Thine heritage, govern them and lift them up forever! Amen!

Chistian News, July 29, 1963

1. God's Church on earth consists of ____.

2. ____ alone makes one a member of God's Church.

3. The Church of the Pope says I ____ on the holy Christian Church.

4. The basic choices among churches are very ____.

5. All non-Lutheran Protestant churches today form one single ____ camp.

6. They all officially deny ____.

7. The divisions in the Reformed camp are mainly about ____.

8. Do most churches today believe they are right and others wrong? ____.

9. The only reason that there is an ecumenical movement is ____.

10. The modern confusion demonstrates the curse of ____.

11. Christ did not found a ____ society for the ____ of truth.

12. Doctrine must be absolutely ____.

13. The true marks of the Church are ____.

14. The Roman Catholic Church is not catholic because ____.

15. The fact that a church body calls itself Lutheran does not mean ____.

16. The L.W.F. welcomes as member churches which ____.

17. The Church of Sweden is in fellowship with ____.

18. Every member church of in the LWF is free to interpret the "doctrinal basis" as ____.

19. The true church is probably statistically always a ____.

20. Pentecostals attack the orthodox church for her ____.

21. A holy pious life is not the mark of ____.

22. Throughout Christian Church history unionists and church-politicians have always appealed to ____ when false doctrine is attacked.

23. What did Ibsen's Pastor Brand say about love? ____.

24. Unionism is doctrinally ____.

25. Both ____ and the ____ put a heavy emphasis on miracles.

26. What is Apostolic Succession? ____.

27. The only Apostolic Succession the Bible teaches is ____.

28. Any "succession" without the pure Gospel is ____.

29. Christians are only to belong to ____.

30. True Lutherans avoid participation in worship with ____.

31. There comes a time when we ourselves must assume ____.

32. True faith obeys ____ not____.

33. Expressions like "he turned for her" are ____.

34. The Antichrist sits not in the Devil's stable but in ____.

EVANGELICAL GRACE
VS. ECUMENICAL PRESSURE

A book review by Kurt Marquart, Toowomba, Australia

Having just finished the Franzmann—Lueking symposium, *Grace under Pressure* (subtitle: "Meekness in Ecumenical Relations"), I must confess to an almost evenly divided reaction. Despite the neat logical scheme, the two parts do not hang together very convincingly. It is not simply that almost any other writer must seem like a "then that which is worse," after draught of rich Franzmann wine; the fact is that the Lueking "Pressure" just does not follow from the Franzmann "Grace."

The exposition of Biblical meekness under aspects of obedience, "weakness" and certitude, is deep, defying, and certainly relevant. Meekness is an indispensable and fundamental characteristic of Christian discipleship, and controls and sanctifies all human relationships of the Christian. Self-evidently the official, called representatives of Christ and his Church are no more exempt from the demands of meekness, than they are from the riches of Baptism!

We self-consciously orthodox and Confessional people particularly need to take to heart this salutary medicine. We cannot excuse our own unlovely attitudes (remember our flesh is no less corrupt than of the liberals!) with the divine rightness of our Cause. Nor dare we confuse our own personal offensiveness with the offense of the Cross.

But is all this really the central problem in interchurch relations today? Is the main trouble really a matter of arrogant and adamant attitudes, as these terms are usually understood? Do we not rather suffer from precisely the opposite malady; from a supine, disobedient, bogus "meekness" which poisons the doctrinal atmosphere with skepticism, even while it, paradoxically, fattens some very unmeek ecclesiastical Establishments?

Ours is an age of sham humility, which seeks to make a virtue of the moral-intellectual bankruptcy of Western Liberalism. This "meekness" comes not from Christ, not even indirectly, but from secular humanism, which knows no absolute objective truth. Intellectual, moral, religious, and political compromise and appeasement are the spirit of the times. Rome, always a shrewd assessor of the times, has recognized the fact. It is to this worldly, defeatist agnosticism, not to the meekness of Christ, that Rome succumbed at its Second Vatican Council. "Triumphalism" was sacrificed not on the altar of Crucified Obedience and Certitude, but in the bottomless pit of guilt and doubt, whence arises the "modern" mentality. False confession was corrected not by true confession, but by discussion, by *Dialogue*!

A Collective Death-Wish

Dr. Franzmann realizes of course, as every great exegete must, that

28

Scripture cannot be interpreted simply in the abstract, without reference to the concrete present. In his sections on obedience and certitude he has certainly provided the foundations for a solid front against that fraudulent "meekness" of our times, which Malcolm Muggeridge has called a "collective death wish." I find myself wishing, however, that this font had been more strongly fortified at certain crucial points - - in which case Pastor Lueking could not of course have used this material as a foundation for his "Ecumenical" house of cards. I can do no more than give a few random examples of the sort of Biblical points which would have better safeguarded the presentation against misappropriation.

"Behold I send you forth sheep in the midst of wolves: be ye therefore wise as serpents, and harmless as doves. But be aware of men . . ." says our Lord in Matt. 10:16. Sober, unsentimental realism, and relative freedom from self-deception are part of the "certitude" of true meekness. This is a very necessary antidote against the chloroform of a know-nothing kind of "meekness". True meekness will never work, for instance, as a bias in favor of mistaking the glittering gold and scarlet of the Beast – Woman (Rev. 17) for the sanctity of the "glorious Church, not having spot, or wrinkle, or any such thing" (Eph. 5:27).

A second point is the whole place of logic and argument in theology. Anything smacking of controversy, disputation, or debate, particularly any effort at clear and exact definition, grates on pietistic nerves, and is quickly branded as unmeek. The Gospel in this view is a wooly, personalistic effusion, which can only be "proclaimed", but never defined or argued about. It is "positive," and has no propositional content. Indeed that word "propositional" may well qualify as the most hated in the entire Liberal vocabulary.

A Sickly Superstition

The sickly superstition - - perhaps a form of American pragmatism? - - certainly has nothing in common with the Bible. Christ Himself used very strict logical argumentation against His opponents. At the Apostolic Council in Jerusalem there was "much debate" (Acts 25:7), just as Paul and Barnabas had already "had no small dissension and debate" with the Judaisers (v.2). Indeed, of the great Apostles to the Gentiles we read (or Sabbaths) he argued with them from the scriptures, explaining and proving that it was necessary for Christ to suffer and to rise from the dead" (17:2,3). And neither Christ nor Paul disdained to exploit even their opponents' own church-political forces against them: Matt, 21:24 ff. Acts 23:6 ff.

No, the Gospel was, is, and always will be controversial. True meekness cannot even wish to reduce it to a slick and safe Stewardship Department platitude!

Finally, are not the "separation" texts, like Romans 16:17, II Cor. 6:14 ff, Hebrews 13:10, relevant to "ecumenical meekness"? Is it not true that the Judaisers, whose error St. Paul commends so fiercely in Gal. 1:8,9, regarded themselves and were regarded as baptized and professing Christians; and that the doctrinal difference between them and Paul were no greater than those between today's "denominations", and certainly far smaller between the gulf of orthodox Christianity and the agnostic humanism which flourishes as the "New Theology" and the "New Morality" in the World Council of Churches?

A Pre-Conceived Ecumenical Scheme

But perhaps such particular considerations are more appropriate to the second half of the book, which is supposed to deal with the application of the principles expounded in the first part. Actually, no such application takes place. What we have is a pre-conceived "Ecumenical" scheme forced into Biblical sounding jargon, in deaf disregard of actual Biblical substance. While chapter five is still quite good, in that it makes true and valid points about meekness within local congregations, the position deteriorates rapidly the higher up the Ecumenical ladder we climb.

Of course misunderstandings are undesirable, and should be removed! But how petty and irrelevant that is in the real situation in Christendom. "After all, these controversies are not, as some may think, mere misunderstandings of contentions about words, with one party talking past the other, so that the strife reflects a mere sematic problem of little or no consequence. On the contrary, these controversies deal with weighty and important matters, and they are of such a nature that the opinions of the erring party cannot be tolerated in the church of God, much less be excused and defended." Thus says, not of course Pastor Lueking, but the Formula of Concord (Rule and Norm) to which he presumably professes allegiance. And the reference is not the great differences between the various churches, but to those which had arisen within the Lutheran Church!

Pastor Lueking nowhere actually says that Missouri should join the World Council of Churches, but he makes that point just the same. Twice, on pp. 87 and 95, the writer approvingly cites official W.C.C pronouncements, and both times he takes them at face value, thereby seriously misleading his public.

The first quotation is from the new Delhi, 1961. Unsuspecting readers would naturally take the reference to "Jesus Christ . . . as Lord and Savior" (In the document quoted by Pastor Lueking) as a Christian confession of the divinity of Christ. Yet not only are there many individuals in the W.C.C member churches, particularly among the leadership, who reject the doctrines of the Trinity and of the Divinity of Christ, but whole churches even oppose these truths. This is documented in the W.C.C's own New Delhi Report, pp. 153 ff. And the W.C.C's secretary, Dr. Visser Hooft, had already long ago gone on record as holding that the W.C.C does not concern itself with how the phrase "God and Savior" is interpreted by member churches. He said this in reply to the Fellowship of Remonstrants (Netherlands), who had objected to that wording and its doctrinal content.

The W.C.C and the Resurrection

The second quotation is from the 1954 Evanston "Message." The brief snippet, which includes the words "that Christ is risen" is taken by Pastor Lueking as evidence of the "Strength of the World Council of Churches." Yet when the Evanston "Faith and Order Report" (one of the tributaries issuing into the final "Message") was being written, "objection was raised to the statement 'resurrection in the body' with reference to Christ, and it has been replaced by the simpler phrase 'the resurrection'". Thus reported the *Christian Century* at the time.

The chief weakness of this part of the book is the total absence of any clear doctrine of the Church. America's "denominational" history is briefly sketched, but in purely sociological terms. The writer seems never to have heard of the Marks of the Church, and their fundamental function in determining fellowship relations. No distinction whatever is made between individual Christians, and false churches and their official representatives as such. This of course is already the failing of Missouri's tragic "Theology of Fellowship". Indeed, one should perhaps ask if this fatal fallacy is not at the bottom of the whole attempt to see "ecumenical relations" under the aspect of "meekness." Granted the fundamental importance of meekness in interpersonal relations, is it really a relevant category when dealing with the official positions and relations between the Church of the pure and distorted misinterpretations of Christianity? This subjective personalistic understanding of the Church necessarily leads to an unprincipled, headlong rush into the World Council of Chaos.

The whole obsession with the Behemoth Church is un-Lutheran. Of course, if with Pastor Lueking (Mission in the Making) one first weighs the scales, damning orthodox Christianity as "scholastic confessionalism", and praising pietistic Liberalism as "evangelical confessionalism" then one is free to participate in the grand illusions of the Ecumenical Movement. No longer is one bound then by any objective basis for distinguishing Christ from anti-Christ. When not the pure Gospel and the Sacraments but Ecumenical mysticism and enthusiasm become the Mark of the Church, but of the dark power working through the "Herr Omnes" (Luther: "Lord Everybody") as well as through the collective papacy of the fashionable theologians.

A Babel of Unscriptural Theologies

"The Word of God shall establish articles of faith and no one else, not even an angel" (Smalcald Articles II/II/15). That is Lutheran. In the Ecumenical scheme of things, on the other hand, it is not the given word which judges and determines the Church, but the prior and given "Church" which determines what the word is! And this is hybris - - the absolute opposite of meekness. Strangely enough Pastor Lueking does not even try to relate to the institutionalized Ecumenical movement lip-service. Obedience? The word is meaningless in such a Babel of unscriptural theologies as the World Council of Churches. "Weakness"? No, in the worldly sense the W.C.C wants desperately to be strong. It meddles in the "United Nations," seeks to pressure the West into maximum appeasement of Communism, and sprinkles Christian phrases on racist, hate inspired policies designed to drive civilization away from Africa. It even mocks the

31

suffering Church behind the Iron Curtain, by hobnobbing in "Christian fellowship" with the creatures and propaganda puppets of their persecutors and tormentors! Such was not the "weakness" of Christ or of John the Baptist! And certitude? A wag already long ago observed by World Council of Churches gatherings usually speak with much hesitancy and uncertainty on questions of theology, in which the delegates are experts, and with much conviction and dogmatism on social and economical questions, in which they are not experts! And what spiritual certitude could one expect in such a welter of views?

Pastor Lueking's reference to G.K. Chesterton, and the point about the Roman Catholic cleaning lady's amazement ("You have baptism, too? How wonderful!") bring to mind Chesterton's brilliant insight into the Internationalist/Ecumenical mentality:

"I have at last begun to realize what the worthy Liberal or Socialist of Balham of Batersea really means when he says he is an internationalist and that humanity should be preferred to the narrowness of nations. It dawned on me quite suddenly, after I had talked to such a man for many hours, that of course he had really been brought up to believe that God's Englishmen were the Chosen Race. Very likely his father or his uncle thought they were the lost Ten Tribes. Anyhow, everything from his daily paper to his weekly sermon assumed that they were the salt of the earth, and especially they were the salt of the sea. His people had never thought outside their British nationality . . . And when I realized that, I realized the whole story. That was why they were so excited by the exceedingly dull theory of Internationalism. That was why the brotherhood of nations, which to me was a truism, to them was a trumpet. That was why the Internationalist was always planning deputations and visits for foreign capitols and heart-to-heart talks and hands across the sea. It was the marvel of discovering that foreigners had hands, let alone hearts. There was in this excitement a sort of stifled cry: 'Look! Frenchmen also have two legs! See! Germans have noses in the same place as we'!"

True Ecumenical Meekness

Finally, compare Pastor Lueking's hackneyed tribute to Pope John XXIII ("one of the prime examples of ecumenical meekness") with this candid and perceptive estimate by a Roman Catholic laymen, in a secular journal. After pointing out that "Catholics right and left, Protestant high and low, Jews orthodox and reform, Hindus, Moslems, monarchs, despot, totalitarians, have joined the chorus of praise," the obituary continues:

"What is, of course, arresting about the phenomenon of a world united for perhaps the first time in history, is that no such unanimity met the death of Jesus Christ, Whom, after all, Pope John struggled merely to imitate . . . Nor does such unanimity, even after two thousand years of reflection, now extend to the appreciation of Christ, Who is still widely reviled, widely despised, universally profaned. The reasons why are complex. But one of that is that Christ, in harder accents than his most recent steward, seemed to be calling upon life based largely upon definition, on a purposive discrimination between good and evil, in the art and the science of which He was, of course, the Divine Teacher; whereas the Pope, although of course in thought, word, and deed an obedient servant of the definite structure of Christianity, dramatized a very different quality, an ecumenicist so lofty that from its high position the particularities of every individual sinner were lost, the distinctive shadows of his profile gone; and so, although the Pope could loathe evil, evil, under his reign, appeared to be a disembodied thing, the kind of thing all of us could join together in loathing with the confidence that we were never being asked to loathe something about ourselves" (*National Review*, June 18, 1963, p. 486).

Yes, as a "definitional structure," under C. F. W. Walther, the Missouri Synod had true ecumenical meekness. It demanded nothing but obedience to the Word of Christ. Those who now in the name of "meekness" dispense from this obedience, and protect the disobedient, are themselves the objects and the agents of judgment; for they are creating a very unmeek system of subservience to human authorities, organizations, by-laws, rules, and regulations!

And the Franzmann - - Lueking volume is so typical of the Missouri Synod's plight: The language of its orthodox poets must serve as a cover for the devices of pietistic Liberalism! Very sad!

Christian News April 17, 1967

1. The Lueking "Pressure" does not follow from ____.
2. Meekness is an indispensable ____.
3. A bogus "meekness" ____.
4. Ours is an age of sham ____.
5. Secular humanism knows no ____.
6. What did Rome succumb to at the Second Vatican Council? ____.
7. False confession was corrected by ____.
8. Scripture cannot be interpreted simply in the ____.
9. What grates on pietistic nerves? ____.
10. The word "propositional" may well qualify as ____.
11. At the Apostolic Council in Jerusalem there was much ____.
12. The Gospel will always be ____.
13. The opinions of the erring party cannot ____.
14. Many individuals in the W.C.C. churches reject ____.
15. The W.C.C. does not concern itself how the phrase ____ is interpreted.
16. The whole obsession with the Behemoth Church is ____.
17. What establishes articles of faith? ____.
18. The W.C.C. seeks to pressure the West into ____.
19. Under C.F.W. Walther the LCMS has true ecumenical ____.
20. What is the Missouri Synod's plight? ____.

SOME ASPECTS OF
A HEALTHY CHURCH LIFE

Sometimes a caricature can, by its very distortion, emphasize a neglected aspect of the truth. Now, Satan, being as Luther said "God's ape," distorts and caricatures God's works. A look at the devil's chapel may therefore on occasion serve to remind us of forgotten aspects of the church of God. Indeed heresies are often but distortions and exaggerations of valid but neglected truths.

As the Papacy is the most baffling religious imitation of the church, so Communism seems to me to be its most ambitious secular counterfeit. Lenin decided long ago that the Party could not afford dandies and armchair revolutionaries, who sympathized with the cause from a safe distance, but were afraid to soil their hands or reputations with a bit of violence. He insisted that all members must submit absolutely to the discipline of the Party. This was carried by the majority in 1903, hence the name "Bolshevik"—Russian for a members of the majority.

This parallels, in a distorted way of course, the total claims of Christ and His church. Christ indeed establishes no human dictatorship, no chain of command, but on the contrary, forbids this (Matt. 20:25 ff.), because he creates new hearts, which, drawn by love and not driven by force, find much greater burdens light and pleasurable (Matt. 11:30). But He claims total commitment, total discipleship, total service (Luke 14:25 ff.). Christianity is not for spectators and theorists, but only for participants and practitioners, all of whom without exception and distinction are consecrated in baptism as full-time priests of the Triune God (Rom. 12:1 ff.; I Pet. 2:9).

Now of course the church was never perfect. But how right, and full, and strong was her life in those early centuries, compared with her own time! What fervent devotion, what confessional courage, what missionary zeal, what capacity for suffering, what holiness of life, what mutual love and fellowship, grace the annals of the ancient church! Apart from the Book of Acts itself, think of the church life that surrounded and supported, and was in turn deepened by, men like Athanasius, Ambrose, and Augustine!

How different the picture is today! Discipline hardly exists. It is less trouble today to belong to the average church than to the average civic or sporting body; at least the latter demand *something!* One can join a church without instruction, then stay away from it all one's life, or use it merely as an aesthetic setting to legalize fornication between divorce courts, and at the end be the object of a touching eulogy—self-composed and tape-recorded if desired! And not only the relatives, but the whole civilized community would be shocked and angry at the mere thought of a church refusing such a "Christian" funeral!

Nor are conditions ideal in the orthodox church. There are smugness, self-satisfaction, satiety, and security—all elements of a carnal conservatism. Zeal for the purity of doctrine is not always accompanied by a corresponding thirst for the living God, for true holiness, for full discipleship in terms of mission outreach and concern to build up the brethren in faith and love. Fellowship is often a theory rather than a practice, and real human needs remain unmet. Callous unconcern and a frigid fear of becoming involved find refuge behind the mask of churchly respectability. Worldliness is rampant, and youth are drifting away.

Some excuse, the widespread looseness as an unavoidable result of the times. This assumes, however, that Christianity is a tender plant which cannot survive is an unfriendly climate without external protection. Yet what could have been more hostile to the faith, than the corrupt, degenerate Roman Empire? Those young congregations in Rome, Ephesus, and Corinth grew without benefit of Victorian manners or other social shelters. The "such were some of you" of I Cor. 6:11 refers to a list of vices that covers as wide a range as the most vulgar of modern big city tabloids! Nothing of the kind! She challenged men uncompromisingly to come out of darkness into the light. Although a guilty paganism professed to scorn the Christians as "haters of mankind," it secretly envied the holy joy and strength which they so evidently radiated. Pleasure-ridden, sin-sick, and desperately unhappy, multitudes flocked for healing to the regenerating waters dispensed by the Divine Physician through His church—and found there not comfortable excuses and easy "acceptance," but the challenge, inspiration, and power for supernatural moral heroism.

In our lax, permissive, rotting culture the church must be the salt (Matt. 5:13) of radical non conformity (Rom. 12:2), not a savorless pulp of "adjustment!" The more she seeks to save her life by fawning upon the reigning idolatries, the more she will lose it! But in losing her life in obedient discipleship, she finds it a hundredfold! Youth in particular are not attracted and held by a service catering to her whims. They yearn for the discipline of high ideals, but despise the cant of their flatters. Nothing is more repulsive and ineffective than the circus of middle-aged ecclesiastics absurdly aping the animalistic sounds and manners of juvenile savages! Converts from street-gangs are won not by this bankrupt lot, but by hearty Pentecostalists who call sin sin, however defective their theology may be otherwise!

Behind the Iron Curtain the line between church and world is fairly clearly drawn, and the terrible discipline of persecutions effectively curbs looseness and smugness. In the West, where the world still largely accords "the Church" the Trojan horse of its approval, we Christians must practice the even more difficult art of self-discipline, according to the infallible rule of the revealed divine will.

The Remedy of Activism

In the last century Mid-Western American Lutheranism made a point of rejecting as unchurchly the "new methods" (e.g. revivalism) of Calvinistic Puritanic sectarianism, with which the older, Eastern Lutheranism had increasingly compromised. Confessionally-conscious Lutherans wanted to build and center their church life on, in, and around the Means of Grace.

In the last few decades many synods of conservative background, now completely Americanized, have been losing their confessional consciousness, and have been freely borrowing "successful" methods from here and there. The aims were often laudable enough. A certain reticence, even lethargy, had to be disturbed and overcome; the vast spiritual resources and energies of the priesthood of believers had to be stimulated, tapped, and put to work. But despite some valid results, the over-all effect needs to be seriously questioned. Is the high-pressured activism of elaborate, almost commercially calculated "Stewardship" and "Evangelism" programmers really the same thing as the vitality of the New Testament church? All the humming and clatter suggest an organizational machine rather than the mysterious organism of the True Vine, whose fruit matures unhurriedly in the life-giving breeze of that Spirit who, whether He rustles gently or roars like a rushing mighty wind, always works in sovereign independence, "when and where He pleases, in those who hear the Gospel" (*Augsburg Confession*, V:2, see also John 3:8)!

Church practice must be, to borrow Major C. H. Douglas's phrase, "the policy of a philosophy," that is, it must be a correct application and embodiment of principle. To dress Methodist principles in the garb of Roman Catholic practices is self-defeating. Neither does the theory sustain the practice, nor does the practice illustrate the theory. Similarly, Biblical, Lutheran theology cannot simply be combined with approaches and practices which have been found "effective" or "successful" in Baptist or Presbyterian settings; the attempt results in a sickly hybrid without powers of reproduction.

Several aspects of the popular activism are clearly traceable not to a natural development of the Lutheran rose, but to an artificial and superficial gilding applied from without. In the first place activism is allergic to doctrine. While paying lip-service to established positions, it is anxious to get on with the job, and shows irritation and impatience in the presence of precision, definition, and controversy. Penetrating into Scripture as deeply as the water-spider into the water (as Luther observed about Eck), activism tends to think of doctrine in terms of slogans and platitudes, and to evaluate its pragmatically, as it promotes or retards the empirical, statistical growth of the organization. Faced with a choice, "Evangelism" will tend to choose the numerical, and "Stewardship" the financial aggrandizement of the organization, over purity or correctness of doctrine. This is of course diametrically opposed to the genuine Lutheran principle, which cannot sufficiently emphasize the prior and crucial importance of the purity of the Gospel as the absolute basis as the center of all Church-life (*Augsburg Confession*, VII). Biblical doctrine must indeed judge the validity of statistical "success" and outward "effectiveness;" but to turn this relationship around is, in essence, to yield precisely to the most insolent demands of the Tempter (Matt. 4:1 ff)!

Another issue is the very appropriateness of the concept of "stewardship" as popularly used. Dr. H.P. Hamann warns against the dangers of legalism in this connection, and concludes:

That there is very little justification, if any at all, for describing the Christian life as a life of stewardship, and that the cause of the Gospel would be well served if the term in its popular connection were forgotten...

No one who took up the New Testament in a search for a word to describe in an all-inclusive way the Christian life could possibly pick on stewardship as that word.[1]

"Stewardship," as a dominant idea, fits much better into Calvinistic covenant theology, than into a genuinely evangelical approach. And in reading actual "stewardship" literature, one is often haunted by the distinct impression that a financial pinch was felt first, and the concern for "raising the spiritual level, etc." came second, and that the growth in spiritual life is desired not for its own sake but to put it bluntly, for its cash value! Of course this is all explained in terms of the needs of "immortal souls," but then so were indulgences! Needless to say, what is at issue is not the church's right to ask for love offerings and sacrifices in Christ's name, but the way of doing this, and its proper place in the total Christian scheme of things.

No intelligent person would deny the need for order and organization in the church. But modern organizationalism tends to exalt soulless techniques, with the result that church work is quantified, depersonalized, and dehumanized. It is a terrible travesty on Christianity, when spiritual life is measured mainly in terms of man-hours, meetings, committees and budget, and only secondarily (if at all!) in terms of the quality of fatherhood, motherhood, humility, purity, devotional depth, doctrinal maturity, compassion, faithfulness in one's calling, and the like. Our modern organizational externalism is really of a piece with the pre-Reformation preoccupation with "childish and needless works, such as particular holy days, prescribed fasts, brotherhoods, pilgrimages, services in honor of saints, rosaries, monasticism, and the like" (*Augsburg Confession*, Art. XX). Instead, we need "publications on the Ten Commandments and others of like import," that we may be "taught to good purpose about all stations and duties of life, indicating what manners of life and what kinds of work are pleasing to God in the several callings." And the Confession adds: "Concerning such things preachers used to teach little." Modern "Stewardship Departments" do not seem to do much better.

For all its busyness, modern activism seems to foster a deadly monotony and sameness which quench the Spirit by forcing all the rich varieties of His gifts and graces (I Cor. 12; Eph. 4; I Peter 4:10 ff.) into the same stereotyped mold. The belief in the efficacy of even minor details of suggested form letters in "E.M.V." manuals, for example, is sometimes nothing short of superstitious, and this in circles which are not very particular about the wording of doctrinal statements. The idea is that certain approaches and methods have been "proved successful" in some "pilot project," and ought therefore to be accepted by all. It is assumed that the glib "public relations" of some central headquarters presents the only valid "image" of the church, and must be no means by contradicted locally. Gifts of the Spirit either fall in line with the "programme," or else they are a nuisance. Activism tends to forget that the Galilean who conquered the Roman Empire was set "for a sign which shall be spoken against" (Luke 2:34), and that He conquered through a church which was "everywhere... spoken against" (Acts 28:22). Had the Apostles been intent, in the modern manner, upon gaining everybody's "good will" by means of a "positive public image," rather than upon faithfulness to their Lord's commission regardless of consequences, it is doubtful whether our century would even have heard of them! Godly polemics and apologetics have always been part of the church's missionary panoply.

The systematic mass approach through committee-directed surveys, follow-up work, etc., no doubt has a place in church life, particularly in our day. But to emphasize this as the only or even the main avenue of "home mission" work seems to me one-eyed and dangerous. The phenomenal growth of the church in antiquity happened in another way. Not officially organized "programmes," but the spontaneous spiritual fervor of the individual Christians and of their congregations made them magnets that attracted the spiritually famished multitudes! In other words, not methods and techniques, but the self-authenticating substance and content of Christianity won the day. If this content no longer fires Christians and their congregations with missionary zeal, then this illness cannot be cured with some methodological bag of tricks. "Vigorous organisms talk not about their processes, but about their aims," observed G.K. Chesterton astutely.[2]

If a congregation's spiritual substance does not sell itself with supernatural naturalness (which of course includes arduous missionary labours), the solution does not lie in high-pressure publicity and salesmanship techniques. This merely compounds bankruptcy with dishonesty. And short-term successes gained in this way turn into long-term failures. The poorly instructed "converts" paraded ceremoniously through the front door, drift away quietly through the back door when the spell of advertisement has worn off or when its glib promises fail to materialize in actual church life. Politics may rely upon the image instead of the reality, and commerce may depend on advertising rather than on the excellence of the product; but the church dare not strive for meretricious "appeal" at the expense of truthfulness and faithfulness (I Cor. 4:2).

Perhaps the greatest danger of activism is its tendency to "unchurch" the local congregation by making it an increasingly dependent agent of a centralized bureaucracy of experts and planners of "programmes." At the same time the Office of the Ministry is secularized into a mainly administrative function. In comparison with the glitter and glamour of regional and national conventions of all kinds and of all sorts of ambitious "projects," the local congregation seems drab and uninteresting. The glory departs from the local altar, and the impression begins to prevail that the "real" work of the church is happening somewhere else. The main task of congregations is to provide the funds for this "real" work elsewhere!

It is my firm conviction that this terrible atrophying of the meaning and function of the local congregation is one of the most basic ills of the contemporary church, that ways and means must be found to restore congregational life to its rightful position as the normal center of gravity in the practice of Christianity, and that the activist approach is a short-sighted and misconceived effort which not only makes matters worse but hides the problem behind impressively elaborate scaffoldings. I am equally convinced that Biblical, Lutheran theology, and it alone, contains the correct solution.

The Means of Grace

The kind of steadfast continuing "in the apostles' doctrine and fellow-ship, and in the breaking of the bread, and in prayers" (Acts 2:42), which the New Testament envisages, can really happen only on the local level, where it is possible for people to keep coming together regularly around Christ's Word and Sacrament. On a regional or national basis this can happen only occasionally, intermittently (quarterly, annually, etc.), rep-resentively, and therefore derivatively. The local "steadfast continuing" is primary and constitutive. It is of the *esse* of the church. Organized groupings above the congregational, or local, level are of the *bene esse* or the *plene esse* of the church.

But if the local congregation is to fulfill its crucial, cardinal role, as the church in its place, its members must have a much clearer and more com-pelling rationale of what happens on Sunday mornings than has generally been the case in recent decades, if not centuries. Where the main congre-gational action is understood as an amorphous agglomeration of arbitrary conventions surrounding a sermon, it will be difficult to convince people of the importance of this vague activity. But where the elliptical shape of the thing stands out clearly, in terms of two clearly understood foci, the Word and the Sacrament, participation will be far more than dutiful com-pliance.

As far as the Word is concerned, the Lutheran Church has never for-gotten Luther's insistence on the absolute primacy of God's Word, doc-trine, and preaching. Actual Bible study must be energetically fostered today. Indeed, the need for full-time Christian schools has never been greater than it is now. The sun of Christian doctrine has set long ago for most of our contemporaries, but our civilization has still been enjoying a kind of ethical afterglow of Christianity. Now even that is vanishing, and the world is sinking into the night of a "scientific" barbarism. Secular ed-ucational systems increasingly reflect the evolutionistic-materialistic-ag-nostic temper of the times. In these circumstances, only full-time Christian schools can supply an adequate Christian education.

Less obvious is the status of the Sacrament. Here many observers be-lieve that the Real Presence, while strenuously defended in dogmatics, has in recent times not placed the central practical role in church life which it had in apostolic, ancient, and Reformation times. This means, however, that the corrective is not something new to be obtained from the modern Liturgical Movement, but something old already given in Biblical, Lutheran theology.

Despite valid insights, the Liturgical Movement is dangerous because of its Romanizing sacramentalism, sacerdotalism, and just plain externalistic ritualism. The view of the Sacrament as something essentially sacrificial, something that we do toward God, rather than vice versa, is fundamentally wrong (Heb. 10). The Office of the Ministry is thought of as some kind of new Levitical priesthood, into which men are admitted not by the call of the congregation, but by the laying on of hands in ordination. This leads to a theory of "Apostolic Succession" in one form or another, since the Ministry in this view can be conferred only by one who is already a member of this self-perpetuating order. It is surprising that Romanizing Lutherans can ardently embrace such ideas, when they are rejected in the clearest possible terms in the *Treatise of the Power and Primacy of the Pope*, especially paragraphs 60-72! To deny the conflict is sophistry. One then has to resort to devices like the assertion that the Confessions contradict themselves, are in need of completion, etc. Wilhelm Loehe distinguished between the Confessions and Luther's own individual view. He admitted that Dr. C.F.W. Walther had Luther on his side, but regarding the Confession he wrote:

> Both sides have appealed to the Symbolical Books. Now even though there exists at least one passage which is written in Walther's (individually Lutheran) sense, the plain sense of particularly some places of the Augsburg Confession yields no necessity to explain them according to one or two passages. The Symbolical Books seem incomplete to me (nicht fertig). Were they complete, then I would not understand how both sides could have appealed to them, which is not the case since yesterday.[3]

In the same letter Loehe writes that he conceded to Dr. Walther:

> Nothing except theological competence and the intellectual consistency of the Lutheran system, but there as now claimed that the Scripture proof was lacking—which he did not regard as important, because he was well able to maintain his exegetical authorities over against me (worauf er kein Gewicht legte, weil er seine exegetischen Autoritaeten mir genueber mit Recht gefuehrt halten konnte)...

Still, it is possible that a one-sided exploitation of Dr. Walther's justified polemics against Grabau's hierarchical aspirations has in practice led to an inadequate "Missourian" view of the Ministry. It is perfectly correct to say that a pastor has no right to lord it over his congregation and to demand conscientious obedience in adiaphora—things neither commanded nor forbidden in Scripture. But charity which must rule in such matters, is a two-way street. It is therefore equally true that congregations may not order their pastors about in adiaphora either. The conception of the pastor as an errand-boy following orders comes from secular democratism, and violates I Cor. 4:1 and are really "managers." The New Testament bishops were not advisory figureheads, like modern ceremonial heads of state, but the real executive officers, or presidents of their congregations. A demoralized, browbeaten leadership that dare not lead, does not make for healthy and vigorous congregations. And unless pastors themselves have the proper respect for their office, they will inevitably degenerate into secularized lackeys of some activistic establishment!

The excesses of the ritualistic tendency have done a great deal of damage, not only in fostering Romanizing ideas and practices, but also in giving a bad name to all liturgical interests. Precisely those who have given up the doctrinal substance of Christianity are often most zealous on behalf of liturgical details of all kinds. There is something spiritually pathetic and pathological about an attitude which freely and indiscriminately mixes up St. Paul, Barth, Augustine, Tillich, Luther, Aulen, etc., but then becomes very conscientious about the requirement that candles must contain at least 51 percent pure beeswax! The devil take their beeswax if they won't leave us Christ's teaching intact!

Yet the ritualistic excesses of our time remind me of a child clawing at walls and eating dirt: there is obviously something missing in his diet! While we have remembered the truth that "ceremonies or church usages... are in and for themselves no divine worship or even part of it,"[4] we have not always remembered the corresponding truth of the *Augsburg Confession* "that nothing contributes so much to the maintenance of dignity in public worship and the cultivation of reverence and devotion among the people as the proper observance of ceremonies in the churches."[5]

The core issue raised by the Liturgical Movement, however, has to do not with ceremonial detail, but with the place of the Lord's Supper in the life of the church. In view of the Movement's aberrations, it can serve us mainly by stimulating us to look to the rock whence we were hewn—the theology of the Scriptures and the Confessions. Here we will find all that is valid in the Liturgical Movement, plus the proper dogmatic foundation, and minus the exaggerations and distortions.

The Lutheran Church has always understood the Liturgy, the main service of the Church, consisting of preaching and the Sacrament, not as a purely historical-traditional development, but as something deriving from the very teaching and practice of the New Testament itself.

The *Apology*, while strongly rejecting the sacrilegious notion that Christ's body and blood are sacrificed anew in the Lord's Supper, admits that the entire action, including the sermon, etc., may be regarded as a sacrifice of praise and thanksgiving (not as a propitiatory sacrifice). In this connection it becomes clear that the *Apology's* concept of the Liturgy is deeply rooted in the theology of the Bible:

> We are perfectly willing for the Mass to be understood as a daily sacrifice, provided this means the whole Mass, the ceremony and also the proclamation of the Gospel, faith, prayer, and thanksgiving. Taken together, these are the daily sacrifice of the New Testament; the ceremony was instituted because of them and ought not be separated from them. Therefore Paul says (I Cor. 1126), "As often as you eat this bread and drink the cup, you proclaim the Lord's death."[6]

Dr. C.F.W. Walther's great edition of Baier's Compendium, approvingly quotes John Gerhard as listing among the "less principal purposes" of the Sacrament:

> 4. That we might preserve the public assemblies of the Christians the strength and bond of which is the celebration of the Lord's Supper. I Cor. 11:20.[7]

Elsewhere Gerhard spells out New Testament practice even more fully:

Because therefore it has been accepted as a practice in the Christian Church, that in the public assemblies of the church after the preaching and hearing of the Word, this Sacrament is celebrated, therefore this custom must not be departed from without urgent necessity...it is...clear from Acts 20:7, I Cor. 11:20, 33, that when Christians did gather at one place, they were accustomed to celebrate the Eucharist.[8]

And Dr. Walther colleague, Friedrich Lochner, wrote in his classic Hauptgottesdienst:

On the basis of Acts 2:42 and I Cor. 11 and according to the example of the ancient church, the Lutheran Church regards the Communion service as the most glorious and important of all public services...She therefore distinguishes between the Main Service and Minor Services. A divine Service becomes the Main Service not by virtue of the significance of the Sunday or the holy Day, nor because of the season of the year, nor through liturgical elaborations, but, as given by the Scriptural relation of Word and Sacrament, by virtue of the fact that the action of the Sacrament of the Body and Blood of Christ immediately follows upon the proclamation of the Word of the Gospel, and thus represents the seal of the Word, the aim and conclusion of the Service. All other services, in which the action of the Sacrament is not intended from the outset, become Minor Services, no matter how rich their liturgical appointments.[9]

Dr. Walther said in a Maundy Thursday sermon:

The first Christians celebrated it almost daily; especially in times of persecution, in order to be daily ready for death...The Holy Supper was regarded as the most glorious divine Armory, in which one receives the most invincible weapons for the spiritual battle...The holy Supper with the body and blood of Jesus Christ is the new Tree of Life, which stood in Paradise, which Christ has now again planted in His Kingdom of Grace.

O adorable, comforting mystery! The holy flesh of God, which the angels adore and the archangels' reverence, becomes a food for sinners! Let the heavens rejoice, let the earth be glad, but still more the believing soul, which enjoys such great gifts![10]

And the great Lutheran historical theologian of our time, Dr. H. Sasse, says of Christian antiquity:

This close connection between the proclamation of the Gospel and the Sacrament of the Altar explains the fact that at all times the Eucharist has been the center of the church's worship and life...Thus this sacrament was in every respect the life of the church. It was never to be separated from the Gospel. The church of the first centuries was the church of the Eucharist. A Sunday, a Lord's Day, was unthinkable without the Lord's Supper. But if ever the church was a preaching church, the church of the Apostles and the Church Fathers was. The same is true of all great periods of the church. The sacrament and the sermon belong together, and it is always a sign of the decay of the church if one is emphasized at the expense of the other.[11]

Certainly the Reformation was one of the very "great periods of the church." Its genuine spokesman, the *Augsburg Confession*, says:

> Our churches are falsely accused of abolishing the Mass. Actually, the Mass is retained among us and is celebrated with the greatest reverence.

And the *Apology* elaborates:

> We can truthfully claim that in our churches the public Liturgy is more decent than in theirs...Every Lord's Day many in our circles use the Lord's Supper, but only after they have been instructed, examined, and absolved.
>
> To begin with, we must repeat the prefatory statement that we do not abolish the Mass but religiously keep it and defend it. In our churches Mass is celebrated every Sunday and on other festivals, when the sacrament is offered to those who wish for it after they have been examined and absolved...
>
> There is nothing contrary to the church catholic in our having only the public or common Mass.[14]

Luther himself, in an opinion dated August 15, 1528, recommended:

> that one or two masses be held in the two parish churches on Sundays or holy days, depending on whether there are many or few communicants....during the week, let mass be held on whatever days it would be necessary, that is, if several communicants were there, and would ask and desire it. Thereby no one would be forced to the Sacrament, and yet everyone would be sufficiently served therein.[15]

Luther never contemplated any other main standard Sunday service than one with both preaching and the Sacrament. Both the Latin Mass of 1523 and his German Mass of 1526 include the Sacrament as a matter of course. In fact in the former work Luther strongly disapproves the Roman custom of omitting the Consecration of Good Friday, which is "to mock and ridicule Christ with half of a mass and the one part of the Sacrament."[16] Three paragraphs later he says: "For properly speaking, the mass consists in using the Gospel and communing at the table of the Lord."

This was standard Lutheran practice for about two centuries. Indeed, some church orders of the sixteenth century (for example, Pomerania, 1563, Liegnitz, 194, Wittenburg, 1559 and 1565, and Muehlenberg, 1540 and 1552) prescribed public admonitions "to frequent reception of the most venerable Sacrament" in case the Supper could not be celebrated for lack of communicants.[17]

The "Old Missouri" *Real Lexikon* by E. Eckhardt, which describes "the Lutheran Order of Service" as "a whole with a fine arrangement of its parts" (*ein Ganzes in feiner Gliederung*) and says that "it is just in the celebration of the Lord's Supper and the Main Service reaches its climax,[19] laconically asserts that the Liturgy was corrupted

1. by the Thirty Years War
2. by those of Spener's persuasion (pietists)...
3. by rationalism.[20]

43

This blight must be overcome in large part by a radical re-appropriation of the practical meaning of the Real Presence. I therefore conclude with three great testimonies to the Sacrament:

Christian Scriver:

> We in no way detract from the other means of grace, Holy Baptism, the Word, and faith: we do not want to sunder what God hath joined together; God also has other foods, besides bread, which, eaten by man, strengthens and preserves his body, yet bread is the noblest. What is begun in Holy Baptism, and through the Word, that is confirmed and as it were completed in the venerable Supper; the highest degree which a baptized and believing Christian can reach in the mystery of fellowship with Christ, is without a doubt the one which is granted him in this holy Meal of Love. And I know nothing that would be more powerful in strengthening and preserving faith, and bringing it to full joy and highest pleasure, than just this Sacrament.[21]

C.F.W. Walther:

> Woe to us, therefore, if we wanted to yield and give in here! Thereby we would be surrendering nothing less than the Holy of Holies of the Christian Church, the Ark of the Covenant and the Mercy Seat of the New Covenant...It is true, my beloved, in the Holy Supper there is given to us no other grace than that which is given to us already in Baptism, in the preaching of the Gospel, and in the comforting Absolution...Accordingly it might well seem as if every person is thereby sufficiently supplied with the treasure of the forgiveness of sins and that it therefore matters little if the Holy Supper with its forgiveness of sins is mutilated or taken from him entirely.

> But this is by no means so. Rather, the Holy Supper is the real crown of all the means of grace which Christ has given to His dear Christendom...O, who can express what a glorious, comforting, heavenly sweet Meal the Holy Supper is? Here the forgiveness of sins is not only preached, proclaimed, promised, assured, and sealed to us, as in the other means of grace, but here Christ at the same time gives His Body and His Blood to His Christians, as the guarantee of it...No, a more precious, incontrovertible divine guarantee there cannot be...Let us not be ashamed of this doctrine, but joyfully confess it, and publically praise it as the most precious treasure entrusted to us.[22]

Charles Porterfield Krauth:

> The Sacramental Presence is the necessary sequel, the crowning glory of the Incarnation and Atonement...

> All theology without exception has had views of the atonement which were lower or higher, as its views of the Lord's Supper were low or high. Men have talked and written as if the doctrine of our Church, on this point, were stupid blunder, forced upon it by the selfwill and obstinacy of one man. The truth is, that this doctrine, clearly revealed in the New Testament, clearly confessed by the early Church, lies at the very heart of the Evangelical system—Christ is

44

the center of the system, and in the Supper is the center of Christ's revelation of Himself. The glory and mystery of the Incarnation combine there as they combine nowhere else. Communion with Christ is that by which we live, and the Supper "the Communion." Had Luther abandoned this vital doctrine, the Evangelical Protestant Church would have abandoned him. The doctrine of the Lord's Supper is the most vital and practical in the whole range of the profoundest Christian life—the doctrine which, beyond all others, conditions and vitalizes that life, for in it the character of faith is determined, invigorated, and purified as it is nowhere else. It is not only a fundamental doctrine, but is among the most fundamental of fundamentals. We know what we have written. We know that to take our Savior at His Word here, to receive the teachings of the New Testament in their obvious intent, is to incur with the current religionism a reproach, little less bitter than if we had taken up arms against the holiest truths of our faith. We are willing to endure it...The Lutheran Church has suffered more for her adherence to this doctrine than from all other causes, but the doctrine itself repays her for all her suffering. To her it is a very small thing that she should be judged of man's judgment...[23]

The church of the pure Word and Sacrament dare not underrate the power and the genuinely religious appeal of the modern "Ecumenical" maelstrom. These forces cannot be met with mere defensiveness. We must have something stronger, better, and more convincing to offer searching youth. The recovery of the full richness of our Biblical-Confessional heritage, and not in a academic, antiquarian way, but as living practice, is therefore a matter of top priority. And we must not allow ourselves to become side-tracked by misunderstandings, as if, for instance, it were a question of the "frequency" of Communion celebrations. Beneath all practical details we must appreciate anew the basic principle that in the extraordinary, but a normal, regular, usual, and integral part of congregational worship. It is, in fact, the New Testament the Holy Supper is not something occasional, additional, or extraordinary, but a normal, regular, usual, and integral part of congregational worship. It is, in fact, the New Testament in action. On this basis a solid, compelling, and convincing local church life can be built. And when local congregations are inspired by a coherent and confident view of their function and dignity, instead of being patronized by centralized ecclesiastical super-corporations and confused by painful uncertainties and anxious experimentings with ever new techniques, the "youth problem" is largely solved, and a firm, integrating principle exists for effective mission outreach.

Awake, Thou Spirit, Who didst fire
The watchmen of the Church's youth,
Who faced the foe's envenomed ire,
Who witnessed day and night Thy truth,
Whose voices loud are ringing still,
And bringing hosts to know Thy will.

O haste to help, ere we are lost!
Send preachers forth, in spirit strong
Armed with Thy Word, a dauntless host,
Bold to attack the rule of wrong:
Let them the earth for Thee reclaim,
Thy heritage, to know Thy name.

The Church's desert paths restore:
Let stumbling-blocks that in them lie
Hinder Thy Word henceforth no more,
Error destroy, and heresy.
And let Thy Church, from hirelings free,
Bloom as a garden fair to Thee.[24]

References

1. H.P. Hamann, "Stewardship and the Gospel," *Australian Theological Review*, Vol. XXXVII, Nos. 2 & 3 (April-September, 1966), p. 57.

2. G.K. Chesterton, *Heretics* (London: Bodley Head, 1960), p. 9.

3. Wilhelm Loehe to Grossmann, letter of July 1, 1853, "Correspondence and Other Papers of the Rev. Wilhelm Loehe, Item 15," in the files of the Concordia Historical Institute, St. Louis, Missouri, U.S.A.

4. Formula of Concord, Epitome, X 3, in T. Tappert, ed., *The Book of Concord* (St. Louis: Concordia, 1959), p. 493.

5. *Ibid.*, p. 49.

6. *Ibid.*, p. 256.

7. C.F.W. Walther, ed., *Joh. Gulielmi Baieri Compendium Theologiae Positivae* (St. Louis: Concordia, 1879), Vol. III, p. 529.

8. Martin Chemniz, Polycarp Leyser, John Gerhard, *Harmoniae Quotuor Evangelistarum* (Frankfurt & Hamburg, 1652), Vol. II, p. 1085.

9. F. Lochner, *Der Hauptgottesdienst der Evangelisch Lutherischen Kirche* (St. Louis: Concordia), p. 6.

10. C.F.W. Walther, *Guadenjahr* (St. Louis: Concordia, 1890), pp. 209 ff.

11. H. Sasse, *This Is My Body* (Minneapolis: Augsburg, 1959), p. 2.

12. T. Tappert, ed., *op, cit.*, p. 56.

13. *Ibid.*, p. 220.

14. *Ibid.*, pp. 249, 250.

15. Martin Luther, *Saemmtliche Schriften* (St. Louis Edition), X, 2256-2258.

16. *Luther's Works* (American Edition), vol. 53, p. 24.

17. F. Lochner, *op. cit.*, p. 7.

18. E. Eckhardt, *Homiletisches Reallexikon* (Blair, Nebraska, 1909), under "*Gottesdienst*," p. 436.

19. *Ibid.*, under "*Abendmahl*," p. 43.

20. *Ibid.*, under "*Gottesdienst*," p. 436.

21. Christian Scriver, *Seelen-Schatz* (Berlin: Evangelischer Buecher-

Vercin, 1864), vol. I, p. 756.

22. C.F.W. Walther, *Amerikanisch-Lutherische Evangelien Postille* (St. Louis: Concordia, 1875), p. 147.

23. Porterfield Krauth, *The Conservative Reformation and Its Theology* (Minneapolis: Augsburg, 1963), pp. 650, 655, 656.

24. *Australian Lutheran Hymn Book* (Adelaide: Lutheran Publishing House), Hymn 240. Vv. 1, 3, 6.

Christian News, August 18, 1969

1. What is the most baffling religious imitation of the church? ____.
2. "Bolshevik" is Russian for the ____.
3. Today ____ in the church hardly exists.
4. Zeal for purity of doctrine is not always accompanied by ____.
5. Who is drifting away? ____.
6. Eastern Lutheranism increasingly compromised with ____.
7. Who has been losing their confessional consciousness? ____.
8. Activism is allergic to ____.
9. Genuine Lutheranism emphasizes the importance of ____ as the center of all Church-life.
10. "Stewardship," as a dominant idea fits better into ____.
11. How did phenomenal growth in the early church happen? ____.
12. The church must dare not strive for "appeal" at the expense of ____.
13. Where does the real work of the church take place? ____.
14. What alone contains the correct solution? ____.
15. What is of the esse of the church? ____.
16. Luther insisted on the primacy of ____?
17. The need for full-time ____ now is greater than ever.
18. The world is now sinking into ____.
19. The Liturgical Movement is dangerous because ____.
20. Romanizing Lutherans are embracing ____.
21. Wilhelm Loehe distinguished between ____.
22. Who is the most zealous on behalf of liturgical details? ____.
23. The devil takes their ____ if they won't leave us Christ's teaching intact.
24. The Lutheran Church regards the Communion service as ____.
25. The church of the first century was the church of the ____.
26. The Apology says that in our churches ____ is celebrated every ____.
27. How does the "Old Missouri" Real Lexikon by E. Eckhardt describe "the Lutheran Order of Service?" ____.
28. What is a matter of top priority? ____.

THE CHURCHLY NATURE OF LCMS

Sir, in response to Dr. Drickamer's "What Pieper Really Said" (CN, 28 July) permit me to state the following: First of all, I appreciate Dr. Drickamer's friendly and collegial sentiments, which are cheerfully reciprocated.

In support of my defense of the churchly nature of the Missouri Synod I had made some seven references to traditional Missouri sources (CN 14 July). Of these Dr. Drickamer ignored five, disputed two, and scored one. In the interests of time and space I shall simply concede the Pieper reference (I, 185) which, in the original, has the word for "church" not as a noun, but adverbially.

On Pieper's main dogmatic treatment in Christliche Dogmatik III, 486-487, however. Dr. Drickamer is mistaken. In this section, entitled "Orthodox and Heterodox Churches" Pieper uses the terms "church" and "ecclesial communion" interchangeably. Footnote 1547 (page 487) defines Pieper's usage with the utmost precision:

> Orthodox churches in our time are the Lutheran congregations and ecclesial communions which actually teach and confess the doctrines presented in the confessional writings of this church, because the doctrines presented (there) are, as an examination shows, the doctrines of Holy Scripture. Impure or heterodox churches are the Roman church, the Reformed church with her many subdivisions, and also the communions calling themselves Lutheran, which do not actually teach and confess the doctrine of the church of the Reformation (my translation).

Item: In his 1916 lectures (*Vortraege*) on Walther's *The True Visible Church*, Pieper writes, for example:

> If there is in Australia a church — and there is, thank God, a church there which agrees with us in the true faith — then we must maintain fellowship of confession and love also with that church (p.161).

Item: Missouri's own official "Brief Statement" confesses:

> 29. The orthodox character of a church is established not by its mere name nor by its outward acceptance of, and subscription to, an orthodox creed, but by the doctrine which is actually taught in its pulpits, in its theological seminaries, and in its publications . . . a church does not forfeit its orthodox character through casual intrusion of errors, provided, etc.

Item: *In Christian Dogmatics III*, 431 (the German text is the same) Pieper cites with approval (naturally!) Luther's definition:

> A church is a group or assembly of baptized and believers under one shepherd, whether of one city, or of an entire country, or of the whole world.

It is of course quite useful to distinguish, as the old dogmaticians did, between "simple churches" or congregations, and "composite churches," or larger bodies. What is, however, perfectly clear is that there is no basis whatever in traditional Lutheran theology, especially Walther's and Pieper's, for denying that "composite churches" are really churches. For good measure, a citation each from the Book of Concord and from Holy Scripture: ". . . decisions of synods (councils) are decisions of the church . . ." (Treatise, 56). In Acts 9:31, the best reading is considered to be "church" in the singular:

"Then the church throughout Judaea, Galilee, and Samaria enjoyed a time of peace."

Yours faithfully,
K. Marquart
Ft. Wayne, Indiana

Christian News, September 1, 1986

1. The LCMS's Brief Statement teaches that the orthodox character of the church is established by ____.
2. Is there any basis in traditional Lutheran theology for denying that "composite churches" are really churchly? ____.

THE LUTHERAN DOCTRINE OF THE CHURCH

Sir,

The Drickamer-Nehrenz symposium on church and ministry in your June 30 issue compels me to respond. The reason is not that Brother Nehrenz mentions me by name and gets almost everything he quotes from me wrong — pre-Convention fever explains but does not excuse the suspension of normal rules of courtesy and care — but that this matter of church and ministry is so vitally important, also in our present Synodical troubles. It simply will not go away till it shall have been properly resolved.

Naturally I am not pretending to be offering the needed solutions. I can do no more than to show that some of the Drickamer-Nehrenz claims are theologically impossible, and then to urge all and sundry to do the serious theological work necessary to reclaim our full confessional heritage in this matter. The merging Lutheran synods have quite forgotten the Lutheran doctrine of the church, and the success-oriented organisationalism in our own Synod is pushing in the same direction.

Two preliminary observations:

(1) Contrary to Brother Nehrenz' impression, I happen to believe, with the late Dr. Wilhelm Oesch, that C.F.W. Walther was the greatest Lutheran ecclesiologist and the most faithful interpreter of Luther in the 19th century debate about church and ministry. The trouble is that not everything given out as Walther's position nowadays really was Walther's position. And before enrolling me, the Ft. Wayne Faculty, the CTCR, and other unlikely co-conspirators in a grand "plan" to subvert Walther's biblical doctrine of the ministry, Brother Nehrenz might have taken notice, for instance, of what I actually hold in the clearest possible language, and in the very booklet he cites repeatedly:

"(Ordination) has nothing to do with the imparting of powers supposedly residing only in the clergy and communicable only by the laying on of hands on the part of those who are themselves already a part of this self-perpetuating clerical caste. On the contrary, the Gospel and all its treasures (Keys, ordination, etc.) belong primarily and directly ('immediately') to the 'whole church' (Tr. 24,68. German), 'because it alone has the priesthood' (Tr. 69) of I Pet. 2:9" (Ministry and Ordination: Confessional Perspectives, p. 14).

(2) I share some of the concerns of both Dr. Drickamer and Brother Nehrenz, e.g. bureaucratic centralization generally, and the lumping together of pastors and teachers into the quite secular (IRS!) category of "ministers of religion," in the proposed Resolution 5-02. But the theological argumentation needs to be sound!

The chief fallacy, as I see it, is the flat assertion: "The synod is not a church." There are no doubt right intentions behind this statement, but as it stands, it is simply indefensible. Consider Pieper's definition: "A congregation or church body which abides by God's order, in which therefore God's Word is taught in its purity and the Sacraments administered according to the divine institution, is properly called an orthodox church (ecclesia orthodoxa, pura)" (Christian Dogmatics, III, 422).

Our synodical fathers simply took it for granted that the Missouri Synod, as a part of the orthodox Lutheran Church, was itself an orthodox church. And so was the entire Synodical Conference, founded in Walther's own life-time, and with the self-understanding of having as its constitutionally embedded "aim and purpose" the "consolidation of all Lutheran synods of America into a single, faithful, devout American Lutheran Church."

Walther's whole book on the "True Visible Church" turns on this understanding, which is simply taken for granted in standard Lutheran writers. Walther's 1870 theses on "Altar Fellowship with the Heterodox" begin like this:

1. The true visible church — in an unrestricted sense — or a part of it, is the one in which God's Word is purely preached and the holy sacraments are administered according to Christ's institution.

2. A communion in which God's Word is in principle falsified, or in which such falsification is in principle permitted, is not a true, orthodox, but a false, erring church or sect.

Clearly, the Missouri Synod, together with its sister churches throughout the world, was understood to be an orthodox church or "communion." That doctrinal unity and church fellowship, not constitutional trappings, were considered decisive, is evident from this quite unselfconscious remark in Pieper : "In this conviction the entire Synodical Conference is by God's grace united and active as one Church" (Dogmatics, 1, 185). And at its 1874 Convention it simply seemed self-evident to the Missouri Synod that "the whole churchly power of the congregations is represented in the Synod when it is assembled" (1874 Report, p. 59).

This last statement clearly illustrates the old understanding: "Synod" is not the organizational scaffolding, the "servant structure," but simply the member congregations, standing and confessing together. Of course the organizational aspect is strictly human, but the unity of faith and doctrine, and the fellowship in the pure Gospel and Sacraments, these are God-given, and it is these God given, heavenly things which shape and determine the Synod's churchly nature. Failing to see the difference between human organization and divine doctrine and fellowship, and the constitutive nature of the latter, Brother Nehrenz wrongly takes me to be saying that the outward Synodical structure is a divine institution. Heaven forbid!

Why then the strong insistence by some that "synod is not a church"? The motive obviously is to prevent ecclesiastical tyranny. What is overlooked, however, is that the logic works in just the opposite way. If with the Reformation one rejects the Roman/Anglican notions of the church as a chain of command, then one must surely be quite clear that the church as church cannot tyrannise anyone. Faith is bound only to the Word of God, and everything else in the church is settled by love and mutual accommodation. The church has no right to bind anyone's conscience one iota beyond God's written Word. It is just the churchly nature of anything that is a guarantee against tyranny, for the church is bound by its divine constitution, anchored to its apostolic foundation (Eph. 2:20), where true spiritual liberty is granted to every son and daughter of God. This was for Walther and Pieper the real reason why the Synod and its members had to be governed by God's Word alone: because that is how Christ governs His church, and not by means of human power and authority (See Pieper 's 1896 Convention essay on "Church and Church Government ," 1896 Report, pp. 27-46).

But if the Synod is not a church, then "anything goes." If, for instance, it is basically a business corporation seeking to market a successful religious "product," then the seeds of tyranny are everywhere. 51 per cent majorities can then behave just as ruthlessly as do similar corporations in Fortune's Top 500! Corporate rat-races of course are fuelled by "effectiveness," not by faithfulness to "old-fashioned" (read: churchly) standards—as though God' s Kingdom were built by our clever methods and techniques rather than by His life-giving Gospel and Sacraments alone, "when and where it pleases Him " (Augsburg Confession V)!

Let us hope and pray that the Indianapolis Convention will help us to remember, not to forget, what it means to be a responsible part of the worldwide, orthodox, Evangelical Lutheran Church!

Yours faithfully,
K. Marquart
Concordia Theological Seminary
Ft. Wayne, Indiana

Christian News, July 14, 1986

1. What did Marquart believe about Walther? ____.
2. The fathers of the LCMS took for granted that the Missouri Synod was a ____.
3. Is the outward Synodical structure a divine institution? ____.
4. If the Synod is not a church then ____.

NAFZGER SAYS AFFIRM AND CTQ PUBLISH FALSE INFORMATION

"Levels of Fellowship" continues to be the topic of considerable discussion within The Lutheran Church-Missouri Synod. Dr. Samuel Nafzger, executive Secretary of the LCMS's Commission on Theology and Church Relations last month told the LCMS's Nebraska District's Spring Pastoral Conference that two conservative publications in the LCMS, Affirm and the *Concordia Theological Quarterly*, published "false and/or misleading information" on the subject. *Affirm* is published by conservatives in the LCMS and the CTQ is published by the faculty of Concordia Seminary, Ft. Wayne, Indiana. Concordia Seminary Professor Kurt Marquart is the author of an article in the CTQ on "levels of fellowship."

Some conservatives contend that LCMS President Ralph Bohlmann and Dr. Nafzger, a loyal supporter of the LCMS president, are seeking some new position on fellowship for the LCMS in order to allow for what the LCMS formerly taught was sinful religious unionism with liberals who rejected basic truths of the Bible. Bohlmann has been denying that the LCMS is now permitting religious unionism. *The Christian News Encyclopedia* documents more than 100 cases of religious unionism which took place in the LCMS while Bohlmann has been president.

Nafzger told the Nebraska District Pastoral Conference: "Much has been written around the Synod on this subject in recent months. I myself have given a couple of papers on this general topic. President Bohlmann distributed a video..."

Nafzger said that articles published in Affirm and in the *Concordia Theological Quarterly*, "have contained false and/or misleading information, have been critical of the very notion of 'levels of fellowship' or 'levels of relationship.'"

Nafzger, as the executive secretary of the CTCR, is a member of a division of the National Council of Churches. According to the NCC constitution, any member of the NCC or any NCC division must recognize all other members of the NCC and its divisions as being "one in Christ" with him and his church body. The NCC admits into membership churches which no longer insist on such doctrines as the deity of Christ and Christ's resurrection. In 1966 it admitted into membership the anti-Trinitarian Swedenborgian New Jerusalem cult. LCMS conservatives maintain that, since the LCMS is not "one in Christ" with the modernists in the NCC or the anti-Trinitarians, Nafzger should get out of the NCC division regardless of what any new "levels of fellowship" doctrine may allow.

LCMS officials, who favor the LCMS membership in an NCC division, maintain that such membership gives the LCMS an opportunity to witness to the NCC and find out what is going on in the NCC. Conservatives have noted that *Christian News* has publicized far more about the NCC than any LCMS publication and has witnessed to the truth to the liberals in the NCC far more than any LCMS official. Conservatives also contend that one does not have to join a liberal organization to witness to its members. "You don't become a freemason to tell them about the Gospel of Jesus Christ" the conservatives observe.

Nafzger told the LCMS's Council of Presidents on March 6:

Professor Marquart, in an article titled "Levels of Fellowship: A Response" in the latest issue of the CTQ. Which arrived at my home on Saturday, March 4, comments on this. While admitting that "The Wisconsin Synod's 'unit concept' is open to serious theological objection" (p. 256). Marquart, nevertheless, seems to hold to a similar position. Criticizing President Bohlmann's video comment that "we have long recognized that there can be various levels of interaction with other Christians, and that the amount or degree of doctrinal agreement is a key factor in determining what we can do together." Marquart says:

> Either there is agreement in the pure Gospel and the right administration of the Sacraments, and then there is fellowship, or there is no such agreement and therefore there is no fellowship. But cooperation in externals requires no doctrinal agreement at all. Can we not freely cooperate with Buddhists and Atheists in various worthy civil endeavors? What has doctrine to do with it? In other words, "levels of fellowship" and the old **insacris-in extermis** distinction define two different and fundamentally incompatible frames of reference or "models" of fellowship. (p. 255)

I disagree with such a "unit concept" view of fellowship. And it is clear that Marquart's real objection to Bohlmann's video is based on his rejection of the very possibility of talking about fellowship relationships with Christians not in church fellowship with one another.

Christian News, May 8, 1989

1. The Christian News Encyclopedia documents more than 100 cases of ____.

2. According to the constitution of the NCC, any members of the NCC or its divisions must recognize all other members of the NCC or its divisions as being ____.

3. What did Professor Marquart say about levels of fellowship? ____.

THE CHURCH AND HER FELLOWSHIP, MINISTRY, AND GOVERNANCE

By Professor Kurt E. Marquart

Reviewed by Pastor Gregory L. Jackson, Shepherd of Peace Evangelical, Lutheran Church-WELS, 1950 Hard Road, Worthington, OH 43235.

[Order from The International Foundation for Lutheran Confessional Research, R.R.3, Waverly, Iowa, 50677-9517. Do not order through Concordia, Ft. Wayne.]

The largest Lutheran denomination in America, ELCA, is struggling with a multi-year study of ministry. The next largest, the Lutheran Church-Missouri Synod, is debating the ordination of women, a topic not even considered by Dr. Franklin Clark Fry, the last president of the ULCA and first president of the LCA. (The LCA did not ordain women until Fry died of cancer.) The third largest Lutheran denomination, the Wisconsin Evangelical Lutheran Synod, is facing related issues, such as clergy resignations. Women in authority over men in the church, and Reformed concepts of ministry. The Evangelical Lutheran Synod recently dealt with receptionism in the doctrine of the Lord's Supper.

Lutherans in America are living with and tolerating the collapse of the orthodox Christian faith. The majority of Lutherans in our country cannot hear a Lutheran pastor who actually believes what Luther taught. Many Lutheran pastors who congratulate themselves for being orthodox routinely mouth such Reformed doctrines as, "We must make the Gospel appealing to people," or "We have to market the Gospel." The Missouri Synod supposedly defeated the historical-critical method of shredding the Bible, but now LCMS pastors throng to Fuller Theological Seminary, where Scriptural inerrancy is openly rebuked amidst signs, wonders, and speaking in tongues.

Lutherans should study Kurt Marquart's *The Church and Her Fellowship, Ministry, and Governance*, to avert the catastrophe which awaits the dissolution of orthodoxy in America. Marquart's volume is a work of genuine scholarship, one which deserves to be studied, re-read, and kept on the bookshelf next to a worn copy of Walther's *Law and Gospel*. Marquart combines an encyclopedic knowledge of the Scriptures, Luther, the Book of Concord, Walther, Hoenecke, and other Lutheran theologians, to give us a complete discussion of the current issues of ecclesiology.

I have known Professor Marquart for five years, attending some of his classes, hearing him at Ft. Wayne conferences, and talking over issues with him informally. Marquart is one of the best classroom teachers in Lutheranism, giving his students more than memorized answers about doctrinal issues. Students leave his class with a love of the Confessions and a thorough knowledge of why the Lutheran Symbols are important in the Christian Church. Marquart is modest, full of humor, and patient with people struggling with issues and not as well informed as he. Marquart is regarded with great affection by his students and fellow faculty members. WELS pastors read The Anatomy of an Explosion, Marquart's painstaking analysis of the Seminex walk-out and the widespread apostasy which preceded it. Both Marquart and Robert Preus are highly regarded among WELS pastors for their courage and orthodox doctrine. Both have suffered for their orthodoxy, but their pruning experiences (John 15:1-8) have made them more fruitful for the Kingdom.

Doctrinal Issues

When discussing his book at the last Ft. Wayne conference, Marquart pointed out that Lutherans have aimed their guns at the Roman Catholic Church to such an extent over the years that infiltration from the Reformed has been relatively easy. (Few Lutheran pastors have "poped," the English expression for joining the Roman Catholic Church. A murmur went through the crowd as people thought of Richard J. Neuhaus, who switched his allegiance from Tietjen the anti-Preus to John Paul II, the anti-Christ.) When Lawrence of Arabia attacked the port city of Qatar, according to Marquart, all the guns were pointed toward the sea, none toward the desert. Marquart said that not only the nose of the Reformed camel is in the Lutheran tent, but "also the very large hindquarters."

Marquart properly begins the discussion of the Church with Christology and uses four models of ecclesiology. Avery Dulles, S.J., who served as sponsor for Neuhaus, started the model language with his *Models of the Church*, now a standard work in ecclesiology. (Dulles' nickname among Catholic priests is "A Very Dull S.J.") Marquart uses four paradigms or models of the church:

1) Eastern Orthodox;
2) Roman Catholic;
3) Lutheran;
4) Zwingli-Calvinist, or Reformed.

Marquart states that Roman Catholicism and Eastern Orthodoxy externalize the Church while Calvinism spiritualizes her. The Lutheran view is incarnational, while Roman Catholics confuse the true church with the visible body headed by the pope. The Calvinists allow the visible and invisible church to stand side by side, without relating the two, like their Nestorian confusion about the Two Natures of Christ (p. 10).

Marks of the Church

Although one might find Reformed leaven thriving in various parts of Lutheranism, the marks of the church (notae in Latin, but Zeichen in German, equivalent to the Johannine miracles) reveal the differences quite easily. The Word and the Sacraments of Baptism and Communion (both Sacraments receiving their power through the Word) are rejected as the Means of Grace by Zwingli, Calvin, and their Protestant and Pentecostal counterparts today. For the Zwinglians (and Calvin in doctrine says little

56

more than Zwingli, only in a more refined way) the Sacraments are ordinances which allow man to do something for God, witness to his faith. They are not God's miracles of today.

Nor do Zwinglians properly teach the Word as a Means of Grace. They believe the Word of God must be polished up and marketed by man's reason or it has no power. It must be defended by man's reason to be of any use. Otherwise, it is "a dead letter." Strangely, Calvin and his heirs teach that the Holy Spirit works apart from the Word, creating a theological puzzle even more mysterious than Calvin's doctrine of the Lord's Supper.

A Roman Catholic priest, observing the daily Mass attendance of a Methodist ethics professor, noted, "He's sacrament-starved, like all Protestants." Those who deny the Sacraments always substitute something else to fill the void. Some make prayer the Means of Grace (inviting Jesus into your heart, as if He cannot come through the Word and Sacraments). Others make tongue-speaking and faith-healing the Zeichen of the Church. Thus, C. Peter Wagner begins his Church Growth classes with hand-waving, tongue-speaking, and "healings," in a vain attempt to show that the true church exists only when the Holy Spirit can be conjured. Yet, Lutheran pastors watch Wagner in awe and emulate his methods, if not always with the same degree of showmanship.

> Accordingly, we should and must constantly maintain that God will not deal with us except through his external Word and sacrament. Whatever is attributed to the Spirit apart from such Word and sacrament is of the devil. Smalcald Articles, Part 111, Article VIII, Confession[1]

One is tempted to think that the Fuller influence is new. But Dr. Conrad Bergendoff wrote in 1956 about frontier Lutherans:

> The European Lutherans had memories of stately church buildings in which a liturgical service of ancient use had been held every Sunday and holiday of the church year. The "American" churches were mostly non-liturgical. They paid little or no attention to the festivals of the ecclesiastical calendar. Their "order of service" was highly fluid, subject to change by the leader of worship. Liturgy was "Romanist," and in the middle of the last century there was a dread of any form of papal invasion. . . Ecclesiastical vestments were taboo. The American church was more tabernacle than temple. Altars were not welcome.[2]

Luther wrote: "The church is recognized, not by external peace but by the Word and the Sacraments.

"For wherever you see a small group that has the true Word and the Sacraments, there the church is if only the pulpit and the baptismal font are pure. The church does not stand on the holiness of any one person but solely on the holiness and righteousness of the Lord Christ, for He has sanctified her by Word and Sacrament."[3]

The marks of the church, then, are not a budget in the black, a net gain of 10 communicants per year, or a Valium haze of happiness. As long as church officials employ business methods to measure the congregation congregation, businessmen in the congregation will be continuously misled into believing that correct doctrine is detrimental to the success of their parish. C.F.W. Walther, who would be unemployed in Lutheranism today, correctly pointed out in *Law and Gospel* that the Missouri Synod grew numerically as a result of correct doctrine and closed his magnificent work with Luther's teaching about the first fruit of a successful pastor: correct teaching. Orthodox teaching gives the glory to God, while all false teaching ultimately gives the glory to man. Thus every Zwinglian-Calvinist denomination has become moderate, liberal, then Unitarian in time.

(Unitarianism is another way of spelling "Tis I ruin a man.")

The Book of Concord states:

> "Likewise, we reject and condemn the error of the Enthusiasts who imagine that God draws men to himself, enlightens them, justifies them, and saves them without means, without the hearing of God's Word and without the use of the holy sacraments." [Tappert— "A marginal note at this point reads: 'Enthusiasts is the term for people who expect the Spirit's heavenly illumination without the preaching of God's Word.'"]

Formula of Concord, Epitome, Article II, Free Will.

If each Lutheran denomination copied the last two pages of *Law and Gospel* and mailed them to each pastor and council member, the vineyard would be fruitful once again. However, the church is being defined as public relations. Doctrinal issues are being avoided. Orthodox Lutheran pastors are being treated as pathogens.

Orthodoxy as Right Praise

Some, especially those tutored by the Pasadena divines, see orthodoxy as an obstacle to be removed in order to promote successful evangelism. For them, orthodoxy is associated with cold, unfriendly congregations, legalistic requirements, and dull worship (a.k.a. the historic liturgy). One should not confuse obnoxious with orthodox, even if both words start with the same letter. Bad attributes come from sinfulness hiding behind dead formalism, not from the Word of God itself, nor from the faithful confession of saints and martyrs before us. Keeping in mind the incarnational nature of the church, orthodoxy can also mean "right praise" as well as "correct teaching." (p. 27)

My boom box is playing a tape of the Russian Orthodox communion service. Except for slight variations, the English words are almost identical to the communion service in *The Lutheran Hymnal*. The worship service is truly the gate of heaven, as this tape shows, offering the love and mercy of God through Christ, both in Word and Sacrament. The historic liturgy, taken directly from the Word of God, is not something to be toyed with or replaced by moralizing and touchy/feely schmooze. Our worship services confess our faith and reveal our loyalties, if we think the Gospel needs our help to accomplish God's will, then we should stand in front of an M1A1 tank in Iraq and protect it from harm with our bare hands.

Fellowship

Another hot topic in Lutheranism is fellowship. ELCA is moving toward

58

complete altar and fellowship with the shrinking Episcopalian Church (membership down from 3 million to 2 million), an urge described as "necrophilia" by one ELCA observer. Worship with non-Christians is discussed seriously in ELCA, and talks with Rome and the Baptists continue. The Missouri Synod seems offended by the conservatism of the WELS and the Evangelical Lutheran Synod, but not by the aberrations of ELCA and other denominations. This is an age which tolerates error but not truth, so fellowship issues are vitally important for all Lutherans.

Fellowship principles are not treated by Marquart as a list of rules to be followed or multiplied. They begin with our relationship to God through worship. Marquart's discussion is very good, but might have included Pieper's distinction about the expression of unity. One might attend a service or wedding or funeral at a heterodox church, but the person would not participate, which would express unity in doctrine where none exists. Organized prayer by clergy (local ministerial associations) is often an expression of unity. Thus, Missouri changed when the gap was widened to allow for various types of unity and cooperation.

The primary problem remains the attitude behind unionism, not the elimination of the fruits of unionism. The attitude is one of indifference toward orthodoxy, as proven by the groupiness of the National Council of Churches. Local ministerial associations, modeling the NCC, organize group Thanksgiving services and Lenten services because they cannot fill their own naves alone, or if the truth be known, together.

Marquart does not support the novel teaching of "levels of fellowship" which reminds so many of the levels of UFO fellowship in the movie "Close Encounters of the Third Kind." Marquart writes: "On the other hand, where heterodoxy reigns, or is given equal rights with orthodoxy, church fellowship must be refused." (p. 61)

Lutheran pastors have faced the issue, or dodged it, in their graduate studies. The argument is: "I am not heterodox just because I attended a liberal seminary." The question remains about whether the person has sufficient discernment to guard against the influence of false doctrine. This is even more true when the school is the trendy place to be and promotes the trendiest of fads. We should study false doctrine diligently, but also pray, "Lead us not into temptation. . ."

Marquart has a fine passage, worth studying, on fanatical recreations to fellowship problems, including the superb story from Luther about the man who stabbed his brother when trying to kill the bear. The point of the story is that the Protestants and Enthusiasts of Luther's day rejected baptismal regeneration as a Roman doctrine, killing the sacrament for fear of the pope. American Lutheranism, under the influence of Revivalism and Pietism then, and Revivalism and Pietism now, has suffered from similar reactions to the liturgy, the clerical collar, and clerical robes (versus the Geneva gown, conveniently renamed "black robe").

Fellowship Is Confessional
Marquart correctly quotes Karl Barth's proud comments on the lack of confessional books in the Reformed tradition. The Lutheran books, accord-

ing to Barth, "possess an odor of sanctity." Marquart writes:

> The decisive impulse here, evident already in Calvin but stronger in Barth, is a deeply Platonic, anti-incarnational spiritualism, which decrees an eternal apartheid between finite and infinite, temporal and eternal, human and divine." (p. 73).

Herman Sasse wrote:

> The means of grace are thus limited for Barth. The preacher descending from the pulpit can never quote Luther and say with joyful assurance that he has preached the Word of God. Of course, he can hope and pray; but he can never know whether the Holy Spirit has accompanied the preached Word, and hence whether his words were the Word of God. To know this, or even to wish to know it, would be a presumptuous encroachment of man upon the sovereign freedom of God.[5]

One hardly needs to wonder why students of Karl Barth, such as Paul Hinlicky and Daniel Fuller, reject inerrancy with such violence and scorn. Schmauk wrote:

> The modern radical spirit which would sweep away the Formula of Concord as a Confession of the Church, will not, in the end, be curbed, until it has swept away the Augsburg Confession, and the ancient Confessions of the Church— yea, not until it has crossed the borders of Scripture itself, and swept out of the Word whatsoever is not in accord with its own critical mode of thinking. The far sighted rationalist theologian and Dresden Court preacher, Ammon, grasped the logic of a mere spirit of progress, when he said: 'Experience teaches us that those who reject a Creed, will speedily reject the Scriptures themselves.'[6]

Confessing one's faith, which began with the Bible, not the Book of Concord, includes both the affirmation of the truth and the rejection of falsehood. (For example: "I am the way, and the truth, and the life. No one comes to the Father except through Me." John 14:6)

Orthodoxy includes both doctrine and practice, just as sincere faith leads to good works. Subscription to Scripture and the Confessions is not sufficient to make a church orthodox, and a church may be orthodox without a formal subscription to the Confessions as the ruled norm. The Francis Pieper quote on this subject, footnoted on page 74, is worth studying. Schmauk wrote:

> The real question is not what do you subscribe, but what do you believe and publicly teach, and what are you transmitting to those who come after? If it is the complete Lutheran faith and practice, the name and number of the standards is less important. If it is not, the burden of proof rests upon you to show that your more incomplete standard does not indicate an incomplete Lutheran faith.[7]

Franklin C. Fry, who was once considered quite liberal in the eyes of other churchmen, (and rightly so, for his principled opposition to inerrancy and to close communion) is quoted by Marquart to show how important fellowship principles were once to Lutherans. Fry stated:

> Insistence upon agreement in doctrine as a precondition for church

60

fellowship is the distinguishing mark of Lutherans among all Protestants and should never be relaxed. (p. 77)

Fry's influence upon the NCC and WCC probably made both groups slide into paganism a bit slower.

Ministry

Lutheran laity commonly confess today that they do not know the difference between the call of a Sunday School teacher and the call of an ordained pastor. An extremely helpful point is made by Marquart in the loss of the word *Predigtamt* (German, preaching office) among English speaking Lutherans. Ministry as an administrative convenience, a Reformed concept, has come into Lutheranism in the form of "lay ministry."

"It is taught among us that nobody should publicly teach or preach or administer the sacraments in the church without a regular call." Augsburg Confession, Article XIV, The Call.[8]

The preaching office (*Predigtamt*) is under fire precisely because the anti-Confessional nature of Reformed doctrine has had so much influence. When "bottom line" church officials undermine the call, wolves move in to murder and steal among the sheep who are no longer being guarded. If pastors are not supposed to divide Law and Gospel, teach the truth of God's Word in spite of the consequences, and administer the Sacraments according to Scripture (i.e. close communion), then members will have great difficulty distinguishing between a Sunday School teacher and a pastor.[9] Then the pastor is just another employee, not worthy of double honor or even single honor. Congregations are more than willing to fire pastors, acknowledging in their practice that they no longer believe in the divine call from God through the congregation. Church officials are more than willing to hold the cloaks for the participants (Acts 7:58).

Church and Ministry

Marquart has provided a useful excursus on Missouri and WELS, Church and Ministry. Old Missouri and Old Wisconsin were not far apart, according to Marquart. However, Graebner's denial that anything other than a local congregation is really church led to all kinds of mischief. "This fostered organizationalism and unionism." (p. 221) Schmauk wrote: "Rationalism, unionism and nativism, both European and American, have been the cause of the bulk of the trouble in the Lutheran Church in America. Perhaps the most insidious and treacherous of these ostensible friends has been unionism."[10]

Sometimes the discussion is used to prove that Missouri cannot have doctrinal discipline because the District Presidents are not really pastors, merely administrative executives. It is also used to prove that only WELS can have doctrinal discipline. Form is not the issue, since some Missouri pastors pursue doctrinal issues according to Scripture. Power is not taken from above, but given from below. The passivity of pastors and congregations has allowed many evils to become entrenched.

The issue was not divisive in the old Synodical Conference. Were that our only issue today!

Ordination of Women

Chemnitz complained in *Examination* that when the papalists were defeated when arguing from the Scriptures, they changed their methods and began attacking the clarity and completeness of the Word of God. Suddenly the Bible was confusing and incomplete, impossible to interpret correctly except through the pope, who grew in infallibility as his office weakened. According to Vatican II, all priests are infallible when teaching the doctrines of Holy Mother Church, another reason for poping.

Another sign of the end is the attack by Lutherans on the clarity and completeness of the Scriptures. Although the Church did not ordain women for approximately 19 centuries, even when a "monstrous regiment" of women ruled Europe, in the words of John Knox, Lutherans suddenly find confusion, disorder, and incompleteness in the passages on the relationship between men and women in the church. First the cultists, then the Pentecostals, then the NCC liberal denominations ordained women. The Lutherans and Episcopalians were last to find cause for ordaining women, and in the case of the Lutherans, it was done over the dead body of Franklin C. Fry.

That women's ordination finds a place in Marquart's book marks the weakness of Lutheranism today. Denominations have shown that a topic which can be debated can also be subverted, which is perhaps why Fry never discussed the ordination of women. Nevertheless, Marquart's material is needed by Lutherans in the continuing debate, which is given credibility by the fact of women preaching to men in Missouri congregations. As Marquart warns, the discussion should not pander to misogyny, even though pressure for women's ordination comes from the secular feminist movement. He might have also added that Missouri's third seminary, Fuller, has no trouble with women theology professors, but does have problems with men who object to such practices. Fuller has a committee for dealing with feminist issues.

Apart from the doctrinal aberrations which quickly follow the impulse behind women's ordination, such as abortion on demand and gay ordination, Missouri can look to ELCA for the practical consequences of changing to neo-Lutheranism. ELCA has a vast pastoral shortage, in spite of doubling the pool of prospective pastors. The seminaries are emptying and pastors are quitting in droves. Some parishes in ELCA and the mainline churches have become "all-female," with a woman pastor and mostly female leadership. Women in these churches have been asked if they like the absence of men, who desert leadership roles as fast as women take them over, according to Church Growth expert Lyle Schaller. The women reply, "We are not happy. We miss the men."

The problem will remain for Lutherans, not in keeping women out of leadership roles, for women are natural leaders in the congregation and will fill a vacuum created by men, but in keeping men in leadership roles. To illustrate: one WELS congregation could not keep its women's group going, due to full-time jobs, school, and all the other reasons. The men formed a men's group, did one activity per month, and suddenly the

62

women's group formed again, larger than ever. The women said: "If the men can meet and get things done, so can we." In WELS and ELS congregations, the women in general have a larger and more important role than in liberal parishes, in liberal parishes, only the feminists have influence. There the hymn parody is especially true:

In the world's great field of battle,
In the bivouac of life
You will find the Christian soldier
Represented by his wife (footnote, p. 168)

Where men worship, study the Bible, and lead the congregation and their families as the head of the household, under Christ, the Kingdom will bear fruit.

Other Considerations

A brief review can hardly do justice to Marquart's scholarship, breadth of knowledge, and clarity of expression. *The Church* will remain a standard for many years to come, replete with references to the standards of Lutheran orthodoxy and contemporary theology. The strength of the study will remain the incarnational basis of the book, always relating ecclesiology to Christology, practice to worship and doctrine. The world scene is not neglected, although this review has omitted many references to Australia, where Marquart served as pastor, and to the Lutheran World Federation, the culmination of doctrinal indifference. I hope that this series, edited by Dr. Robert Preus, will do for Lutheran orthodoxy what C. Peter Wagner has done for the "spiritual gifts industries." (p. 133) Marquart's *The Church* sold 800 copies in the three weeks following its debut.

Footnotes

1. *The Book of Concord*, ed. Theodore G. Tappert. Philadelphia: Fortress Press, 1983 p. 313.
2. *The Doctrine of the Church*. Philadelphia: Board of Publication, ULCA, p. 48.
3. *What Luther Says*. I, p. 263.
4. *The Book of Concord*. ed. Theodore G. Tappert, Philadelphia: Fortress Press, 1983, p. 471.
5. *Here We Stand*. trans. Theodore G. Tappert, Minneapolis: Augsburg Publishing House, 1946, p. 161.
6. Theodore E. Schmauk and C. Theodore Benze, *The Confessional Principle and the Confessions*, as Embodying the Evangelical Confession of the Christian Church. Philadelphia: General Council Publication Board, 1911, p. 685. [Schmauk was the president of the (conservative) General Council, 1903-1918. The influence of the conservatives led to the ULCA merger in 1918. Afterwards, the liberals took over. The General Council never resolved Masonic lodge membership, pulpit and altar fellowship with the Reformed, and millennialism. These "open questions" were the crack through which all the hobgoblins of liberalism entered.]
7. *The Confessional Principle and the Confessions*, p. 890.
8. *The Book of Concord*, ed. Theodore G. Tappert. p. 36.

9. "Is the Lord's Supper the place to display my toleration, my Christian sympathy, or my fellowship with another Christian, when that is the very pool in which most of all we differ; and in which the difference means for me everything — means for me, the reception of my Savior's atonement? Is this the point to be selected for the display of Christian union, when in fact it is the very point in which Christian union does not exist?" Theodore E. Schmauk and C. Theodore Benze, *The Confessional Principle and the Confessions*, pp. 985f. 10. Ibid, p. 855.

Christian News, April 1, 1991

1. The LCA did not ordain women until ____.
2. Lutherans in America are tolerating the ____.
3. Marquart combines an encyclopedic knowledge of ____.
4. Marquart is one of the ____.
5. Richard Neuhaus switched his allegiance from ____ to ____.
6. Who rejects the Sacraments as a means of grace? ____.
7. Luther wrote that the church is recognized by ____.
8. Orthodoxy includes both ____ and ____.
9. According to Marquart, Old Missouri and Old Wisconsin were ____.

CONGREGATIONAL CHURCH GOVERNMENT

Sir,

Herewith some concluding thoughts about polity—I have no wish to bore your readers with a permanently revolving door on the subject.

Our historic polity is best called "congregational self-government." There are two sides to this, a spiritual-theological, and a civil-temporal. Spiritually, theologically, our congregations stand together as one confessing church in the Synod. We were not founded to be hundreds or thousands of independent little local sects, each with its own "foreign policy," i.e. fellowship arrangements. Our doctrine and confession is (supposed to be) one. If a congregation dissents from the Synod's uncompromising adherence to the Lutheran Confessions—as expressed for instance in the *Brief Statement*—it must ultimately go elsewhere. But in a congregation's own local, internal affairs, the Synod is purely advisory. Of course, when we still had an independent adjudication and appeals system, it used to be customary to include in congregational constitutions the provision that in case of division over doctrine, the property would belong to that party which continued to adhere to the true doctrine of Scripture and Confession.

Spiritually, theologically, no error has the slightest right of existence in the church. Any decision contrary to the Word of God as rightly confessed in the Book of Concord is null and void. No resolution, no matter how unanimously passed by congregations, commissions, or conventions, has the least validity, standing, or binding force if it is contrary to Scripture and Confession. Such a resolution must be resisted, opposed, treated as invalid, and ultimately reversed by all who recognize the truth, for "we ought to obey God rather than men" (Acts 5:29).

Legally or civilly, on the other hand, any religious body has, under the First Amendment, the right to maintain whatever nonsense and humbug it wishes, so long as no one's rights are violated. As a legal corporation a congregation is perfectly free to vote itself out of an orthodox Lutheran synod, and to be independent, or to join any other body it wishes, even one which uses the Lutheran name fraudulently, while compromising the Lutheran confession in all directions. So, to repeat, morally and spiritually, no one has any right to violate the divine truth by a hair's breadth, "for we can do nothing against the truth, but for the truth" (II Cor. 13:8); but legally a corporation is free to confess or not to confess whatever it wishes. Any "voter supremacy" that cannot handle this vital difference is beside the point.

Congregations are properly self-governing when they let Christ in His revealed Word decide all matters of faith, and let love and mutual accommodation do the rest. And these congregations are not simply groups of individuals, but are (divinely) ordered organisms, consisting of both hearers and teachers. Further, contrary to the fantasy that in matters of customs and ceremonies ("adiaphora") the pastor simply has "one vote, like everybody else," the fact is more complex: both preachers and hearers have something much more important than "vote," and that is "voice." Luther wrote somewhere that one wise old man, citing relevant Scripture, achieved more to settle consciences and convictions at a great council than did all the great bishops and theologians put together. Wise speaking ought to guide all voting. All Christians must act according to their lights here, but pastors have a special responsibility to maintain good, churchly customs:

. . . the authority to establish in outward or indifferent things directions and rules or definite ceremonies for order and propriety as well as to foster agreement among the members of the congregation for public worship or also to abolish them, as this is demanded by the need or benefit of the church. But these powers belong to the whole church and [are not peculiar—*propriae]* to the clergy . However, we readily admit that the first and chief parts of this power pertain to the ministry of the church (John Gerhard, quoted in C.F.W. Walther, *Church and Ministry,* p. 318).

Peace and Joy!
Kurt Marquart

Christian News, May 29, 2000

ECUMENISM: FACTS AND ILLUSIONS

The words "ecumenical" and "ecumenism" come from a Greek word meaning "the whole inhabitable world." The "Ecumenical Movement" means to unite into one worldwide church all the scattered bits and pieces of Christendom. In itself, that is a noble aim. Everything depends on understanding the problem of Christian unity and division realistically. Otherwise, we are likely to apply Band-Aids to cancers, and actually make matters worse.

The Lord makes His church ONE not in just any way, but only in the TRUTH (St. John 8:31-32; 17:14-17). Without real unity in the One Lord, the One Faith, and the One Baptism (Eph. 4:5), mere outward togetherness is a sham. This is why our Augsburg Confession demands for the "true unity of the church" nothing more and nothing less than "that the Gospel be preached unanimously in its pure understanding, and the Sacraments be administered in accord with God's Word." It is not necessary that human customs and traditions be everywhere alike. And, of course, there are believers, dear children of *God,* in all churches which retain enough of the Gospel to make possible the creation of faith.

The three basic confessions or versions of Christianity are the Roman Catholic/Eastern Orthodox, the Lutheran, and the Calvinist (Presbyterian, Baptist, etc.). The differences among these are not minor matters but go to the heart of the Gospel. Did Christ earn for us the free gift of eternal life, as the Bible teaches, or only the opportunity to earn this life by doing good works with His help, as Rome says? An honest reading of Romans and Galatians will leave us in no doubt about the answer. Again, does Holy Baptism give life and salvation, as Christ and His Apostles teach (St. John 3:5, Tit. 3:5, 1 Peter 3:21), or is it only a symbol of our obedience, as the Baptists say? And does the Lord really give us His holy body and blood to eat in His Sacrament for the forgiveness of sins, or is all this only picture and symbol? There is no generic "Gospel," which might overlook or bypass such questions. Any honest confession of faith must "come clean" on matters so clearly taught in God's Word (Gal. 1:6-8).

The modern "Ecumenical Movement" — despite some promising beginnings a hundred years ago —has largely given up on the issue of truth. It concentrates on getting everyone together outwardly, under compromise formulas like the recent "Lutheran" reaction joint statement on justification. During a major seminar on Christian-Muslim relations conducted recently at a "Lutheran" seminary, one person raised the issue of Christian evangelism among Muslims. He was told that this was "facism"! And the Southern Baptists were accused of promoting "ancient hatreds" by proposing to do mission work among non-Christians. This intolerant secular "tolerance," with its fear and contempt for the whole idea of truth, has had its impact also in the churches. And since the bureaucracies and seminaries of the "mainline" churches have given up the authority of the Bible as the Word of God, they, of course, have no grounds for any firm convictions about anything.

Genuine ecumenism must go another way. It must walk by faith, not by sight. That means being guided by the truth of God and not by outward numbers or prestige. Whatever is not built on the one foundation of the apostles and prophets (Eph. 2:20) is to that extent not the church of Christ, but a counterfeit. There cannot be real peace between the Cross of Christ and the wisdom of this world (1 Cor. 1 and 2). As Christians we are called to be friendly and peaceable among people of all kinds — and to love even our enemies. But we cannot go along with a deceitful outward show of church union and communion when there is no agreement in the life-giving doctrine of Christ and His Apostles, on which everything depends (St. John 6:63; Acts 2:42; I Tim. 4:16). The true ecumenical task is to raise everywhere — humbly but with conviction — the banner of Christ's truth and doctrine, and not to budge from it. Such faithfulness God will bless — and is blessing throughout the world today. From Siberia and Kazakhstan to Haiti, from Sudan to Kenya and South Africa, from Europe and Canada to South America and Australia, everywhere the sheep of Christ hunger for the pure Bread of Life and rejoice in it. Thanks be to God!

Concordia Theological Seminary Pilgrimage
Kurt Marquart

Christian News May 29, 2000

1. Lutheranism's historic polity is best described as ____.
2. If a congregation can't accept the Brief Statement then it should ____.
3. In a congregation's local affairs, the Synod is purely ____.
4. Spiritually, theologically no error has ____.

For the Sake of Christ's Commision

CHURCH GROWTH MOVEMENT THREATENS UNITY OF LCMS

"In this generation, the unity of the Synod is threatened by diversity of doctrine and practice originating from influencing that have their sources in Evangelicalism and the Church Growth Movement" says "For the Sake of Christ's Commission," a report of the Committee of the Lutheran Church-Missouri Synod.

Members of the study committee are:

Pastor Phill Andresen, Immanuel Lutheran Church, Spirit Lake, Iowa;

Pastor Jack Baumgarn, Trinity Lutheran Church, St. Francis, Minnesota;

Pastor John Domsch, Hope Lutheran Church, Topeka, Kansas;

Dr. Robert Kuhn, First Vice-President Emeritus, Concordia University, Irvine, California;

Professor Kurt Marquart, Concordia Theological Seminary, Fort Wayne, Indiana;

Dr. Dale Meyer, Lutheran Hour Speaker, St. Louis, Missouri;

Pastor Howard Senkbeil, Elm Grove Lutheran Church, Elm Grove, Wisconsin;

Dr. Gene Edward Veith, Concordia University, Mequon, Wisconsin;

Dr. Richard Warneck, Concordia Seminary, St. Louis, Missouri; and

Pastor Kenneth Wieting, Luther Memorial Chapel, Milwaukee, Wisconsin.

The report says:

"The Gospel and the Sacraments of Christ are the saving treasures of the church. Faithfulness to this Gospel, by which alone the church lives, must remain the central concern of Christ's church on earth. The Lutheran Church-Missouri Synod has been blessed by the use of these treasures. The enemy of God and of mankind, however, has never allowed this Gospel to remain unopposed.

"In a previous generation, the unity of the Missouri Synod was shaken by controversy over the divine authority of Holy Scripture (formal principle). By the grace of God, the Synod emerged from that struggle with a clearer confession of the inspiration and authority if the Bible.

"In this generation, the unity of the Synod is threatened by diversity of doctrine and practice originating from influences that have their sources in Evangelicalism and the Church Growth Movement. Here the content of the Gospel itself is at stake (material principle). Therefore, we address below numerous theological and cultural issues vis-à-vis the Church Growth Movement in the hope that the Synod's mission and evangelism ministries may ever be faithful to Biblical and confessional teaching.

"While earlier studies on this topic have been presented to the Synod,

69

this study is in response to the request of the 1995 Synodical Convention (Res. 3-09, see p. 35). In order to complete our assigned task, this committee divided into two groups, one concentrating on theology and the other on the culture. Our report reflects this division of labor. This document seeks to define 'Church Growth' in the words of the leaders of the movement itself. It also aims to address some of the effects of American Evangelicalism and the Church Growth Movement on the public confession and worship life of the LCMS that have emerged in the past decade.

"Faithfulness to the Great Commission shapes the continuing mission of Christ's church until He comes again: 'Go and make disciples of all nations, baptizing them in the name of the Father and of the Son and of the Holy Spirit, and teaching them to observe all that I have commanded you. And surely I am with you always, to the very end of the age.' (Matthew 28:19-20).

"This report is offered to further the cause of Christ-centered church growth and genuine evangelism . The principles it sets forth should serve to sort out helpful strategies from those that, however unintentionally, obscure the life-changing Gospel of Jesus Christ."

"What Is the Church Growth Movement?

"The growth of the church is by no means synonymous with the 'Church Growth Movement,' anymore than, for example, 'education' is the same as the ' National Education Association.' The Church Growth Movement may not be defined simply as any plan or suggestion to promote the growth of the church. Rather, it is a particular historical development, marked by particular dates, leaders, books and characteristics."

"According to Christianity Today, the movement's 'basic book' is Donald McGavran's 1970 Understanding Church Growth. McGavran, who was a long-term Disciples of Christ missionary in India, tried to reassert the primacy of evangelism in an ecumenical setting that had largely forgotten it. The1990 version of his book was revised and edited by C. Peter Wagner, McGavran' s successor as leader of the movement. The *Christianity Today* article cites Wagner's conclusion: 'I don't think there's anything intrinsically wrong with the church-growth principles we've developed, or the evangelistic techniques we're using. Yet somehow they don't seem to work.' He sees 'Third Wave' neo-Pentecostalism as the solution. Elsewhere Wagner had paid tribute to Robert Schuller, who in turn is indebted to Norman Vincent Peale. Wagner states:

"Possibility thinking boils down basically to a synonym of what the Bible calls 'faith.' Schuller's definition of possibility thinking is 'the maximum utilization of the God given powers of imagination exercised in dreaming up possible ways by which a desired objective can be attained.' He is convinced that 'the greatest power in the world is the power of positive thinking.'

"In his foreward to Carl F. George's Prepare Your Church for the Future (1992), C . Peter Wagner hails the volume as 'the most significant step forward in church-growth theory and practice since 1970.' The book advocates the 'meta-church' concept, which 'highlights the lay-led small group as the essential growth center,' so that 'everything else is to be con-

70

sidered secondary to its promotion and preservation.'

"This book and other Church Growth literature and materials have exerted enormous influence on the official and unofficial mission and evangelism thinking of the Missouri Synod and its districts. See also Kent Hunter's recent defense of the Movement in his Confession of a Church Growth Enthusiast (1997) and the numerous endorsements by LCMS leaders contained in the book."

"The goal of many Church Growth proponents, to win souls for Christ through the Gospel, is a worthy one. Ironically, many of the Church Growth techniques work instead to undermine the Gospel. Church Growth principles have roots in American revivalism, which suggests that people have within them the freewill to ' make a decision for Jesus.' This implies that gaining new Christians is a human work—a matter of rhetorical and emotional manipulation, applying the correct techniques, and following the right principles—rather than the work of God. Typical Church Growth techniques minimize the Means of Grace, which are God's way of conveying the salvation of Christ, and instead confuse Law and Gospel, mingle the Two Kingdoms, and promote a theology of glory over the theology of the cross. Such things, however sincerely done, undermine the very Gospel they are intended to proclaim."

"It follows that the church's mission is to be viewed theologically rather than sociologically.

"Therefore, it is spiritually harmful:

"When an artificial tension is postulated between the church's worship and the church's mission.

"When mission is shaped mainly by its attractiveness and friendliness to unbelievers, thus pandering to the old Adam.

"When secular culture in one way or another controls the shape of the church's mission.

"When multi-cultural emphases override the one transcultural mission of the church to all people, thus promoting a different Gospel for each subculture.

"When the decisive criteria for the church's mission become techniques of commercial marketing, rhetorical persuasion, statistical success, or external appearances of happiness or harmony.

"When recently popularized small groups (meta groups) are viewed as foundational in mission. (Foundational gatherings, or the 'house churches' referenced in Acts 2:42-46 were apostled gatherings of Word and Sacrament ministry.)"

"God's people are a glorious priesthood (priesthood of all believers), which is far greater than and different from the new idea of 'everyone a minister.' The public Gospel ministry , in turn, serves this priesthood of all God's people."

"Therefore, it is spiritually harmful:

"When it is taught that worship is essentially 'celebration' rather than receiving the mercies of Christ in His Word and Sacrament.

"When man-centered ceremonies replace God-centered worship.

"When orders of service are subjectively devised quite independently from orders of worship that are the property of the church universal and that faithfully confess and receive the presence of Christ in His Word and Sacrament.

"When the church's preaching, teaching, music and worship are changed to be more like the world in order to be accepted by the world.

"When the church's solemn public worship is treated as a matter of experiment and entertainment.

"When the loving God-given practice of close(d) communion is abandoned for the sake of perceived friendliness, inclusiveness in worship and numerical growth.

"When so-called "liberty" in worship ceremonies, customs and rites leads to orders of worship that compromise our confession (FCX). The Divine Service includes those rites that confess the saving presence of the risen Christ in His Gospel, such as confession and absolution, Law and Gospel preaching, Creed, the Lord's Supper, prayer for the church universal, etc. (Ap. XXIV).

"When music and hymnody used in worship focus principally on human sentiment and emotion rather than on the Biblical content of the Christian faith.

"When well - meaning pious language is substituted for the historic creeds of the church.

"V. The Lutheran church has a distinct confessional identity.

"The three Ecumenical Creeds (Apostles, Nicene and Athansian) are to be upheld, and initiatives to alter, amend, or replace them with contemporary compositions must be resisted.

"The Ecumenical Creeds articulate the faith confessed by the church universal, as opposed to the teachings of heretics and sectarians (FCE p. RN.3).

"Because the language and expressions of the Creeds have been carefully refined, any change in words or phrases may result in distortion or loss of the life-giving truths confessed so clearly by the church down through the ages.

" When the Ecumenical Creeds are subject to individualized reformulation, they are no longer ecumenical nor are they what they have been for centuries, a tried and true doctrinal standard.

"Preaching and teaching provide the opportunity for presenting Lutheran Confessional identity in the contemporary context.

"The name Lutheran should be retained among congregations of the Lutheran Church-Missouri Synod because 'Lutheran' signifies not a cultic following of Martin Luther but rather fidelity to Christ and His Word (Preface to the Book of Concord).

"It follows that Lutheran distinctive should not be eliminated in favor of a generic Christianity.

"Therefore, it is spiritually harmful:

"When the name and confession known as 'Lutheran' is replaced by a generic Christian identity, which may include heterodox teaching and practice.

"When the name Lutheran is removed from our churches, jeopardizing the visibility of some of the key teachings of our Biblical confession, such as the real presence and compromising conscientious Lutheran pastoral care exercised in the loving Biblical practice of close(d) communion.

"When a generic Christianity downplays controversial Biblical truths in favor of a least-common-denominator approach to doctrine, practice, and fellowship, thus compromising Christ's mission on earth (FCSDX, 5-7).

"When pastors or congregations presume to change or alter the wording of the Ecumenical Creeds to suit their local circumstances."

"I. The Lutheran Theology of the Two Kingdoms teaches that God reigns in all cultures, but that the church is to be ruled by the Word of God alone, and not by the culture."

"It follows that the culture is not to set the agenda for the church.

"Therefore, it is spiritually harmful:

"When the church changes its teachings to follow prevailing cultural trends.

"When theology is determined by cultural considerations rather than by the Word of God.

"When worship is shaped not by theology but by currently popular styles.

"When Christians ignore their responsibilities to serve their neighbors and to apply God's moral law in the cultures in which God has placed them.

"When Christians believe that only 'church work' is a valid way of serving God, so that they neglect their earthly vocations.

"When the church is operated as a purely secular corporation, with the pastor functioning as the 'C.E.O.,' the elders being reduced to a Board of Directors, and the congregation treated as workers, all organized according to a business plan to market a product.

"When the 'Priesthood of All Believers' is taken to mean 'every member a minister.' This view denigrates the secular vocations (in implying that everyone ought to be engaged in ministerial functions to serve God, as if their existing callings were not equally spiritual in God's sight). It also can be used to denigrate the pastoral vocation (in implying that everyone can do what the pastor has personally been called to do)."

"Today's postmodern culture denies that there are any absolutes. Truth is relative; morality is relative; and religion is nothing more than a privatized, interior meaning-system with no connection to transcendent realities."

"III. Cultural pluralism does not mean cultural relativism; rather, it means that the church has the opportunity to reach out to human beings in all of their God-given diversity."

"The fact of cultural diversity does not mean that truth or morality are relative; rather, all cultures are limited in their knowledge, tainted by sin, and are in need of the transcendent truths of God's Word."

"Preaching is theological.

"A sermon must always be the proclamation of the Law and the Gospel, in which God Himself promises to work in a powerful way.

"It is being said by some Church Growth proponents that 'people don't want to hear about sin;' they want a more positive, affirming message that builds up their self-esteem. This approach eliminates the Law. Since 'self-esteem 'theology encourages faith in oneself—rather than in Christ—it also eliminates the Gospel."

"Technology is cultural.

"The advance of the Reformation was greatly aided by the invention of the printing press, the technological innovation that made it possible for everyone to own and to read the Bible. By the same token, other technological developments should be gladly embraced by the church as ways to help fulfill its mission.

"The LCMS was a pioneer in using radio and television to spread the Gospel. Today, the Internet and other information technologies hold great potential for use by the church.

"We can agree with Church Growth experts on such things as the need for plenty of free parking, which is merely an acknowledgment of the importance of transportation technology in contemporary American culture.

"Teaching is technological.

"If there are no moral absolutes, if God's Word is not objectively true, if religion is no more than a private, interior consolation with no reference to a transcendent, universal reality—as today's culture tends to believe—then Christianity is completely invalid. The teaching of the church, in this cultural climate, must be more thorough, more intentional, and more wide-ranging than ever."

Christian News, January 22, 2001
The entire report was published on pages 13-15 of the January 22, 2001 Christian News.

1. The unity of the Lutheran Church- Missouri Synod is threatened by ____.

2. What are the saving treasures of the Church? ____.

3. What should remain the central concern of Christ's church on earth? ____.

4. What is the Church Growth Movement? ____.

5. Church Growth leader C. Peter Wagner said that church growth principles don't seem to ____.

6. Many of the Church Growth principles work to ____.

7. Do people have a free will to "make a decision for Jesus?" ____.

8. Typical Church Growth techniques minimize ____.

9. The priesthood of all believers is far greater than the new idea of everyone is ____.

10. It is spiritually harmful when man-centered ceremonies replace ____.

11. Should close(d) communion be abandoned? ____.

12. The ecumenical creeds articulate ____.

13. The name Lutheran should be ____.

14. Should culture set aside the agenda for the church? ____.

15. Is "church work" the only valid way of serving God? ____.

16. Can everyone do what the pastor has been called to do? ____.

17. Post-modern culture denies that there are ____.

18. Culture pluralism does not mean? ____.

19. A sermon must always ____.

20. The advance of the Reformation was greatly aided by ____.

21. The LCMS was a pioneer is using ____.

THE MARKS OF THE CHURCH

For the Life of the World

Why does the Church need "marks", and what are they? St. Paul says "concerning Christ and the church": "This is a great mystery" (Eph. 5:32). Comments Luther: "...this is a great mystery to be apprehended by faith. It is not visible or tangible; therefore it is a sacrament, that is, something secret, a mystery, invisible, hidden" *(Luther's Works 41:164)*.

The Church is the mystical body of Christ, consisting of all who are joined to Him by God-given faith. It is the Holy Temple growing upon the foundation of the apostles and prophets (Eph. 2:20. 21). Such things cannot be seen by our eyes at present. We see no one Holy Church of Christ. Believers who "have washed their robes and made them white in the blood of the Lamb" (Rev. 7:14). Instead we see various factions and everywhere sinners like us. By faith, we know that we are justified, pure, holy, spotless before God for the sake of Christ, but we certainly see no such thing anywhere on earth, in this life. The Church then is an article of faith, not of sight. As we say in the Creed: "**I believe one** holy Christian Church." Not: "I see one holy Christian Church." What we see is in fact a Churching mass of religious organization, bureaucracies, activities, and individuals of very "uneven quality," to use that favorite phrase of book reviewers. Yet within this mass, we believe the one Holy Church to be hidden—hidden so deeply that "no human reason can find her, even if it were to put on all spectacles" (Luther).

That's why the Church needs identifying signs or "marks"—otherwise we'd be at the mercy of any and every fanatical delusion calling itself "Christian". Here is the classical "marks" language of the *Apology of the Augsburg Confession*:

"However, the church is not only an association of external (things) and rules like other civic organizations but it is principally an association of faith and the Holy Spirit in the hearts of persons. It nevertheless has its external marks so that it can be recognized, namely, the pure teaching of the gospel and the administration of the sacraments in harmony with the gospel of Christ". (Arts. VII and VIII. 5. Kolb-Wengert, p.174) Or:

Nor indeed are we dreaming about some platonic republic... Instead, we teach that this church truly exists, consisting of true believing and righteous people scattered through the entire world. And we add its marks: the pure teaching of the gospel and the sacraments" (par. 20 p. 177).

In other words, only God sees who is really in the Church, for only He can see the faith of the heart. **We can be sure where the** Church is by attending to her marks. Where the Gospel is purely preached and the sacraments are rightly, that is biblically, administered, there the Church comes to its true, proper, and legitimate expression. The more the preaching and sacraments in a given church deviate from the biblical

76

truth, the less certain we can be of the Church's presence there. So long as enough of the Gospel remains for the creation and sustenance of faith, Christians, that is the Church, will exist within such a body: but a body that mixes the Gospel with contrary doctrine, that is, with error and falsehood, is a conglomerate of Zion and Babylon, and lacks the divinely-willed orthodox (right-teaching) character of the Church (see Rom. 16:17).

But why preaching and the sacraments? Because only faith makes one a member of Christ and thus of His Church, and only the Gospel can create that faith. Preaching and the sacraments are simply the various forms of the one Gospel which alone gives life and salvation. See, for instance, Rom. 1:16 and 10:17. This is the evangelical, biblical understanding of the matter. By contrast, others want to identify the Church by all sorts of human devices and traditions, such as grandiose ceremonies and rituals, or allegedly divinely-instituted church bureaucracies and chains of command, especially the so-called "apostolic succession," that is, the allegedly unbroken historical line of ordinations running all the way from the apostles to present-day bishops. All such pomp and circumstance are trivial by comparison with the real "apostolic succession", faithfulness to apostolic doctrine. An "episcopate" that throws biblical authority and basic Christian morality to the winds, and , contrary to the express apostolic prohibition, purports to ordain women into the office of the Gospel ministry, is unapostolic and has no meaningful claims to "apostolic succession". Mere outward, historical ties to ancient places and churches do not count (1 John 2:19). Only faithfulness to the truth counts. After all, a fossil of a fish looks remarkably like a fish, and its stone particles stand in full "anatomical succession" to the particles of the fish—but the thing hasn't been a fish for a long time!

Only the Lord's life-giving words of truth create saving faith (St. Jn. 6:63, 68, 8:13, 32). Every other teaching contradicts and attacks faith. Therefore the Lord—far from urging His followers to treat contradictory teachings with "mutual respect",—in fact warns earnestly against false prophets (Mt. 7:15: 24:11, 24)! Only His Word gives life, and therefore only His Word has any rights in the Church. The apostles likewise allow no contradiction to the one evangelical truth (Acts 2:42; Gal. 1:6-9; Tit. 3:10: etc.).

Perhaps the recent terrorist attacks on New York and Washington can serve to illustrate the point. Everyone is of course, (rightly) horrified at these atrocities, and churches and churchmen are publicly aghast. Yet in their own domain these churches and churchmen smile benignly—not to say inanely—at the ghastliest spiritual atrocities! Once the FBI have identifies the perpetrators of the recent mass-murders, what should we then expect? Would it be a wine-and-cheese reception at which President Bush and the terrorists discuss their differences in the spirit of good-will and "mutual respect"? Surely not even the silliest sentimentalist would expect that! Yet that is the order of the day in the surreal world of "ecumenical" decorum, where every heresy is a legitimate "point of view", and every false prophet a "dear brother in Christ"!

The marks of the Church mean that we are to be guided by faith, not by sight, in dealing with the Church. In the Church, it is above all truth and truth alone that counts—not numbers or prestige or pleasant relations. Where the Gospel is purely preached and the sacraments are rightly administered, there Christ's Church is rightly and properly represented. Any contradiction of the Savior's pure Voice and teaching (St. Jn. 10, "My sheep hear My voice") misleads and **misrepresents the Church, and therefore cannot** be granted any spiritual rights or legitimacy by any church wishing to be "apostolic". Christ's truth unites and divides. Where the priority of His Gospel truth and agreement in it are not valued, it is no use prattling much about "missions," or human, bureaucratic togetherness and "love". It is all a sham. To overlook and make light of false doctrine is to compromise and flirt with the Arch-Terrorist, who seeks to deceive and destroy with his lies (Jn. 8:44, 2 Thess. 2:7ff). But unlike the commercial towers of New York or Washington's pentagon, Christ's Holy Church is so firmly founded on the Divine Rock, that the very gates of hell shall not prevail against her (Mt. 16:18). Thanks be to God!

Christian News, November 19, 2001

1. Christians confess in the Apostle's Creed I ____ in the Holy Christian Church, not ____ one Holy Christian Church.
2. Only ____ faith makes one a member of Christ and thus of His Church.
3. ____ truth unites and divides.
4. Without the ____ all talk about bureaucratic togetherness is ____.

"Nicht Zeitweilig" Not Temporary

THE MINORITY IS CORRECT

CTCR Abandons LCMS Opposition to Temporary Calls

Lutheran Church-Missouri Synod President Jerry Kieschnick has widely circulated "Theology and Practice of 'the Divine Call'", a report of the LCMS's Commission on Theology and Church Relations.

The report has many fine statements. Yet it has some serious weaknesses as CTCR members Dr. Kurt Marquart, Pastor Walter Lehenbauer and Paul Nus observe in their minority reports. This issue includes the Marquart-Lehenbauer minority report. They write that the CTCR document "abandons our Synod's 150 years-long opposition in principle to 'temporary calls'; and (2) in general, we are concerned about a pragmatic type of theologizing which always seeks to reshape doctrine to fit existing practice, rather than correcting practice by the unchanging standard of biblical doctrine."

More than 40 years ago LCMS officials and Concordia Seminary, St. Louis argued that when "regular call" is listed in Article VI "conditions of membership" in the LCMS's constitution this meant that an LCMS congregation could only call a graduate of Concordia Seminary who had been certified by the seminary faculty (Bylaw 6.163). Trinity Lutheran Church of New Haven, an LCMS congregation which called the editor of CN to be its pastor, argued that "regular call" means what is said in Article XIV of the Augsburg Confession: "It is taught among us that nobody should publicly teach or preach or administer the sacraments in the church without a regular call." The congregation noted that the by-laws being used by LCMS officials and Concordia Seminary were not in existence when the LCMS constitution first listed "regular call" as a condition of membership. The original constitution in German said that "regular call" was "nicht zeitweilig" (not temporary).

LCMS officials and Concordia Seminary demanded that Trinity Lutheran Church of New Haven retract its call to the CN editor and send him back to New York. When the congregation asked for reasons, the LCMS officials and seminary refused to give reasons. They acted as if the call extended to the editor was some sort of temporary call which should be withdrawn.

Reprinted below is the transcript of a meeting at Trinity Lutheran Church, New Haven, when the top officials of the LCMS's Western District (now Missouri) demanded that Trinity, New Haven get rid of its pastor. The transcript reveals why the Marquart-Lehenbauer minority report is so important.

Note what Dr. William Beck, translator of **An American Translation**, said at the meeting about marriage and the call. Liberals who controlled the LCMS kept changing by-laws in their drive to get rid of Trinity and its pastor. They insisted upon the absolute binding nature of their man-made laws. CN has complained about a "by-law mentality" in the LCMS for more than 40 years. The Benke case again has shown how the Benke-Kieschnick, Jesus First group relies on man-made by-laws rather than the Word of God. LCMS Vice President Wallace Schulz wrote in a letter with his opinion on the Benke case: "Through their erroneous dependence on man-made documents, some leaders of the LCMS have forced our beloved Synod into the greatest crisis in its history: Will the LCMS build its future on God's Word or men's opinions?"

Laymen at Trinity New Haven said virtually the same thing in 1962. Note what August Korff told the LCMS officials when they visited Trinity: "Will you advise the congregation then to obey men rather than God? Because we cannot dismiss Otten unless he violated God's command. What do you want us to do with him? Obey men rather than God." (Korff lodge at Camp Trinity, New Haven, is named after August Korff).

When Concordia Seminary Professor Alfred Rehwinkel, one of the few seminary professors who had the courage to defend Trinity, heard Korff testify at a meeting of an LCMS Board of Appeals, he said Korff's testimony was wonderful and thoroughly scriptural.

Rehwinkel said he helped write some of the by-laws in the LCMS's Handbook but that because of the unique situation and the liberalism at the St. Louis Seminary against which Trinity's pastor rightly protested, what God's Word says about the divine nature of the call comes before any man-made by-laws. Rehwinkel knew that the seminary refused to certify Otten because Otten had exposed the theological liberalism of various professors. These professors later left the LCMS and formed Seminex.

District officials with the encouragement of liberals at Concordia Seminary banned Trinity's pastor and lay delegate from attending communion at a district convention held at Concordia Seminary. District President James Kalthoff ruled in 2001 that whatever the district officials said about Trinity's pastor not attending communion in the past at district conventions still stands.

During the December 20, 1962, meeting members of Trinity asked why members of the congregation had been banned from communion at district conventions and later other LCMS churches. Top officials of the LCMS declared that members of Trinity were guilty of impenitence of sin and therefore not eligible to take Holy Communion in other LCMS churches. The congregation is supposed to have sinned when it called Otten. Missouri Synod Lutherans were also warned not to take Holy Communion at Trinity Church. In response to an inquiry in 1963, after Trinity was expelled from the LCMS, Dr. Oliver Harms, president of the LCMS, wrote: "You ask whether the members of Trinity Lutheran Church at New Haven can be permitted to communion in our church. The answer is no, they are no longer in fellowship.

"You ask whether the congregation committed a sin. The answer is yes, and the sin is that they refused to live by laws which they voluntarily subscribed to when, at their own request, they became members of The Lutheran Church-Missouri Synod.

"You ask whether or not you might attend communion at Trinity of New Haven. The answer is, you would be out of order and not complying with our position on fellowship by attending communion at Trintiy of New Haven.

"Your question as to how this whole congregation can be suspended and yet others can be permitted to go free and are not disciplined, let me say that in the first place the entire congregation is guilty of violating its own principles and the principles of the Synod which they voluntarily subscribed to, and in the second place men which you mentioned are not guilty of such a sin, and if they are guilty of any, they are under discipline. However, it would be said that neither of the two men you mentioned (Martin Marty and Robert Hoyer ed.) are currently under discipline. The one, Pastor Marty, has frequently expressed himself to be willing to cooperate wholeheartedly with the Synod of which he is voluntarily and happily a member."

Dr. Marty later left the LCMS and in 1992 said that the LCMS and Concordia Seminary had "gone to ashes." Trinity of New Haven petitioned the 1967 convention of the LCMS to ask Dr. Marty to resign as editor of the *Christian Century* since this publication regularly attacks the basic doctrines of the Christian faith and promoted abortion, homosexuality and situation ethics. LCMS officials defended Marty and saw no reason why the LCMS's "shining star" should resign as an editor of the Christian Century. LCMS officials still allow Marty to preach and commune in LCMS churches. He is invited to speak in LCMS colleges and at the LCMS Seminary where Otten has been banned.

Members of Trinity were banned from communing in LCMS churches because they insisted on defending what God says in His Word about the divine nature of the call and for refusing to regard their call as some "temporary call" which could be broken when church bureaucrats ordered that it be retracted.

Dr. Kurt Marquart is one of the few conservatives who has had the courage to speak out against "blatant injustice" in the case involving Otten and Trinity. He wrote in the July, 1998 Reporter: "For the convention to pronounce the Herman Otten case 'closed' (again!) would be to perpetuate blatant injustice and to signal a shameful kinship with corrupt power cliques which habitually punish whistle-blowers rather than wrongdoers."

Christian News, July 21, 2003

1. Regular call in Article VI of the LCMS constitution means ____.
2. LCMS Vice-President Schulz wrote that through their erroneous dependence on man-made by-laws some LCMS leaders forced the LCMS into ____.
3. Dr. Alfred Rehwinkel knew that Concordia Seminary, St. Louis refuses to certify Otten because ____.
4. Dr. Martin Marty said that the LCMS had gone to ____.
5. Dr. Kurt Marquart wrote in the Reporter that corrupt power cliques habitually punish ____ rather than ____.

MARQUART AND LEHENBAUER SUBMIT MINORITY REPORT

Kieschnick Commends New CTCR Statement On Call

"The document abandons our Synod's 150 years-long opposition in principle to 'temporary calls'; and (2) in general, we are concerned about a pragmatic type of theologizing which always seeks to reshape doctrine to fit existing practice, rather than correcting practice by the unchanging standard of biblical doctrine" say Dr. Kurt Marquart and Pastor Walter Lehenbauer in a minority opinion on "Theology and Practice of the Divine Call." This document by The Lutheran Church-MissouriSvnod's Commission on Theology and Church Relations was recently sent by LCMS President Jerry Kieschnick to "Pastors, Teachers, Deaconesses, Directors of Christian Education, Directors of Christian Outreach, Directors of Parish Music, and Congregations of The Lutheran Church-Missouri Synod."

Kieschnick, who had been chairman of the CTCR, says in an accompanying letter. "I believe that the Commission's overview of scriptural and confessional practices and their application to contemporary questions will greatly help the members of the Synod as together they develop call procedures that serve, above all, the ministry of the Gospel and sacraments in faithfulness to the Holy Scriptures and Lutheran Confessions."

Contrary to Kieschnick, the Marquart-Lehenbauer minority opinion says: "If adopted, the new theology would be the first official break - foreshadowed, to be sure, by decades of loose practice - with our Synod's previous stand on the matter throughout its history. Indeed, the whole Synodical Conference from the beginning held that 'the toleration of temporary calls for pastors' was a 'practice contrary to the confession, and therefore a bar to church fellowship' (CTCR Report Theology of Fellowship, p. 20)."

The minority opinion takes issue with what it calls the CTCR's latest document "situationism." The opinion says: "Serious theology needs constantly to call the church's practice back to the pure standard of her doctrine. It is a mark of decline when theologizing is used instead to justify loose, pragmatic practice." "We call upon the CTCR to be more intentionally independent of organizational givens, in order to assert and maintain the sole sway of the divine gift of truth in His holy Word, as purely confessed in the Symbolical Books of the Evangelical Lutheran Church." The entire Marquart-Lehenbauer minority report is in this issue.

Another minority report by CTCR member Paul Nus concludes: "Let us not deprive congregations and pastors of those loving relationships. Every congregations faces its own unique circumstances. It has ever been so. Yet the scriptural theology and practice of the Divine Call has stood the test of time and proven itself over centuries of church life. When we honor the divinity of the Call and uphold what God clearly intended for the good of His church, God's Name is kept holy among us, and we help to ensure that the Gospel has free course in our midst"

THEOLOGY AND PRACTICE OF "THE DIVINE CALL?" A MINORITY OPINION

By Dr. Kurt Marquart and Pastor Walter Lehenbauer

There are of course many fine statements in this CTCR's report, the text of which has been developing in committee for nearly ten years. Our main reservations about this draft are twofold: (1) Specifically, the document abandons our Synod's 150 years-long opposition in principle to "temporary calls"; and (2) in general, we are concerned about a pragmatic type of theologizing which always seeks to reshape doctrine to fit existing practice, rather than correcting practice by the unchanging standard of biblical doctrine.

(1) "Temporary Calls"

Although the document admits that "there have been good and solid reasons for regarding the calls of parish pastors as open-ended or of unspecified duration" (38), and even takes this as normal practice for ordinary parish calls, the document treats this as no more than a desirable a*diaphoron*: "It may well be the case that the length of service, like location and salary, is also an issue that is entrusted to the church to administer 'by human right' (*de jure humano*) (37). Walther says the opposite: **"the church cannot create a call according to its own discretion but can issue only that call which God has instituted and which He alone recognizes (through which alone a servant of God comes into existence, not, however, through a human contract for a few hours and days)"** (*Walther Speaks to the Church: Selected Letters*, Carl S. Meyer, ed. [St. Louis: Concordia Publishing House, 1973], 58; emphasis added).

Indeed, the whole Synodical Conference from the beginning held that "the toleration of temporary calls for pastors" was a "practice contrary to the confession, and therefore a bar to church fellowship" (CTCR Report *Theology of Fellowship*, 20). Unlike other CTCR reports, merely recommended by the Synod for study, etc., this one was formally "adopted" as its position by the Synod in 1967).

If it is true that the minister of the Gospel is "God's man" (1 Tim. 6:11; 2 Tim.3:17), who may therefore be removed from office only for cause (ungodly doctrine, ungodly life, incompetence), properly established (1 Tim. 5:19), then a temporary "call" is simply an enabling device for arbitrary dismissal on unbiblical grounds, and is no call at all. It is in fact "an abominable disorder" (see Walther, below). That is the historic Lutheran position defended by our Synod.

The document's "situationism," which holds that "pastors in specialized fields of service" may be treated differently (38-41), threatens the distinctively Lutheran understanding that there is only one divinely established Gospel ministry, and that all Gospel ministers--whatever their particular specializations--are therefore essentially alike as incumbents of one and the same God-given office. Thus Walther, refuting Grabau's claim that he had the right to dismiss his assistant, Pastor Hochstetter, because he was

83

technically only an "archdeacon," accused Grabau of "sacrilege" and "church-robbery," saying:

"However therefore Pastor Grabau may twist and wiggle, he will never manage to prove from God's Word that there is more than one divinely instituted office, and that there exists a type of preacher who by divine right would be something other or more or less than other [preachers], which of course is a doctrine which domineering pastors would only too fondly like to smuggle in from the Roman or the Episcopal church into the Lutheran (*Der Lutheraner*, vol. 23, no. 9 [1867],67)."

If "the free and unhindered proclamation of the whole counsel of God has been a fundamental reason why the call of a local pastor has been considered permanent" (38), it is difficult to see why that same logic should not apply in other situations. If anything, academic or bureaucratic pressures for conformity within the synodical structure are likely to be much more intense than public opinion within a local congregation. Why then does the document favor temporary appointments or "a rolling contract" (40) for Gospel ministers in such situations? If permanent calls for local parish pastors are desirable in resisting the pressure . . . for the pastor to become a "people-pleaser"" (38),then how can pastors in the employ of the Synod under "a solemn Call" be expected to "serve at the pleasure of the appointing authorities" (1989 *Proceedings*, 129)?

We recognize of course that there are unusual and "fluid" situations. This, however, is not the place to offer detailed suggestions for various cases. What is important is the principle that the one Gospel ministry is conveyed by a regular (non-temporary!) divine call, and that this is also the way for orderly transfers of Gospel ministers from one field of service to another. Within a permanent call to a mission field, for example, orderly changes of location may well be made by mutual consent. And as for elected offices, if they require ministers of the Gospel, then these may either be called permanently or else be given temporary auxiliary calls in addition to their regular, permanent calls. Where there is a will to follow proper churchly practice, there will always be a way. The proposed document's treatment of the new concept of "intentional interim ministry" (see 40-41) does not face up sufficiently to the underlying issues of principle. Nor do the issues of "Resignation and Retirement" (45-46) appear to have been sufficiently thought through.

The majority document is mistaken in assuming (20) that unlike Walther, Pieper "was willing, however, to distinguish between a call for temporary assistance and a temporary call." In point of fact, that distinction had been made already by Walther: "Those preachers, however, who without giving up the office to which they have an orderly, regular call, serve another congregation for a time as it were 'on loan,' with the agreement of their congregation, by no means thereby make themselves guilty of conducting the office on the basis of a temporary call" (*Pastoral theologie*, 4th ed., 1897, 44n). Walther cites biblical and Reformation examples, including that of Bugenhagen, "who near the beginning of the Gospel was lent from Wittenberg to Brunswick for a year."

(2) Doctrine and Practice: The Horse-and-Cart Problem

Serious theology needs constantly to call the church's practice back to the pure standards of her doctrine. It is a mark of decline when theologizing is used instead to justify loose, pragmatic practice. In this way unsound practice ultimately leads to unsound doctrine, instead of sound doctrine being allowed to cure the ills of unsound practice. It is easy for the church, especially in an age of pragmatism, to drift into loose practice. In call matters all sorts of practical anomalies have arisen, and have been accepted apparently without any serious theological analysis. For instance, the Wichita Convention (1989), contrary to Augsburg Confession XIV, accepted Word and Sacrament ministry by uncalled, unordained ("licensed") persons, largely on the grounds that the thing was happening anyway and should be regulated for the sake of good order (1989 *Proceedings*, 111-114). The process that led up to this action, incidentally, had bypassed the CTCR--causing the latter to express official "regret" (April 22, 1989).

We call upon the CTCR to be more intentionally independent of organizational givens, in order to assert and maintain the sole sway of the divine gift of truth in His holy Word, as purely confessed in the Symbolical Books of the Evangelical Lutheran Church.

ATTACHMENT: THE HISTORIC LUTHERAN REJECTION OF "TEMPORARY CALLS"

1992 Resolution 3-09A mandating the study of the Call expressly stated that this was to be done "utilizing the writings of C.F.W. Walther (i.e., his book *Church and Ministry* and essay 'The Congregation's Rights [sic] to Choose Its Pastor'" (1992 *Proceedings*, 116). The intent clearly was to take seriously the balanced, historic, orthodox Lutheran consensus on church and ministry, for the clear exposition and defense of which Walther is rightly famous. The CTCR's document fails to do justice to standard Lutheranism's rejection of "temporary calls," as the following citations clearly show. (Our translations; boldface added).

C.F.W. Walther, *Church and Ministry*, trans. J. T. Mueller (St Louis: Concordia Publishing House, 1987), 311.

Kromayer: "The minister may not be engaged by those who call him through a contract for certain years or with the reservation to dismiss the freely called person. **God nowhere has granted or permitted those who call the right to make such a contract. Hence, neither the one calling nor the one who is called may regard such a call or dismissal as divine**" (*Theologia positivo-polemica*, part II, p. 530).

C.F.W. Walther, *Amerikanisch-Lutherische Pastoral theologie [American-Lutheran Pastoral Theology]*, 4thed., 1897, 41-45, passim.

Especially here in America there exists in many congregations the custom that preachers are called only *temporarily* (for a time), that is, either with the proviso that they may be dismissed at will, or that they are called only for a certain term, perhaps for one or several years, or "until notice," so that they must resign within a fixed time from the day of the notice;

even if all this [includes] the possibility of being elected again for a new fixed term. **However, neither is a congregation entitled to issue such a call, nor is a preacher authorized to accept it. Such a call is before God neither valid nor legitimate. It is an abuse [Unsitte]. It conflicts in the first place with the divinity, clearly certified in God's Word, of a true call into a preaching office in the church (Acts 20:28; Eph. 4:11; I Cor.12:28; Ps. 68:12; Is. 41:27).** For if God is actually the One Who calls preachers, then the congregations are only the instruments for the selection of the persons for the work to which the Lord has called them (Acts 13:2). Once this has happened, the preacher stands in God's service and office, and no creature can then deprive His servant of his office or dismiss him, unless it can be proved that God Himself deprived him of his office and dismissed him (Jer. 15:19, cf. Hos. 4:6), in which case the congregation does not really depose or dismiss the preacher, but only executes the manifest deposal or dismissal by God. If the congregation does that nonetheless, then it, the instrument, makes itself the mistress of the office (Mt.23:8, cf. II Tim. 4:2, 3), and interferes with God's rule and administration, whether [such congregation] makes arbitrary decisions about this already before or during the call, or whether it presumes to do so afterwards. But the preacher who gives a congregation the right to call him in this way, and to dismiss him at will, thereby makes himself a hireling, a servant of men. **Such a call is not at all that which God has ordained in respect of the holy office of preaching, but is an entirely different matter, which hasn't got anything to do with it. For it is no mediate call through the church, but a human contact; it is no life's calling, but a passing function outside the divine order; an ecclesiastical, thus a human order, or rather an abominable disorder made contrary to the order of God. It is therefore, as stated before, without any validity, null and void, and one so called is not to be regarded as a servant of Christ and of the church.** Such a call conflicts also, secondly, with the relationship in which congregation and preacher are to stand towards each other according to God's Word. It conflicts firstly with the *honour* and the *obedience*, which the hearers are to show the administrants of the divine office of preaching according to God's Word (Lk. 10:16; I Tim. 5:17; I Thess. 5:12, 13; I Cor. 16:15; Heb. 13:17); for if the hearers really had that alleged plentitude of power, then it would be fully within their power to withdraw themselves from the divinely required observance of that honour and of that obedience. No less is every sort of a merely temporary call also contrary to the *faithfulness and constancy* until death which God requires of preachers (I Pet. 5:1-4; I Tim. 4:16; I Cor. 4:1 ff.) and contrary as well to the *accounting*, which the preacher as guardian over souls will one day have to render (Heb. 13:17). Finally a temporary call is contrary both to the *practice* which the Lord commanded the *apostles*, and which they observed, according to which they, namely God's Spirit through them, not the hearers, had to determine how long they would and should remain with a congregation (Lk. 9:4, 5), and also contrary to the *practice of the church* in those times when corruption in doctrine, life, order, and discipline had not set in. That, incidentally, with the existence of that sort of call the church can nevermore be rightly cared for or governed, or the right discipline be practiced, or the church be rightly grounded in the faith and in pious ways, and be propagated, requires no proof; **such a call opens gates and doors to all disorder, confusion, and all mischief through gainsayers and through men-pleasing and men-fearing belly-servers. . .**

Finally, Ludwig Hartmann writes: "Here belongs also that controversial question, whether someone may consent to render his service or official work to the church *for certain years*. We say no: 1. Because such a calling impertinently prescribes to God, Who calls, a certain time, after the lapse of which he will depart from that church, no matter how it might behave; as it is not the place of a legate to prescribe to his lord how long he is to represent him. 2. Because *fleshly counsels* are at hand, which ought to be far away; for such an one thinks that if things don't turn out according to his heart's desire, if no treasures are to be gathered or many adversities to be endured, then he will easily disentangle himself from these labyrinths. 3. For the sake of many *disadvantages*: for if the faithfulness of a pastor were very pleasing to the church, she would suddenly be robbed of it; also because through such frequent changes the property of the church is much diminished, as is well known. If one now asks further, whether it is permitted to *call* a servant of the Word *under the definite condition of how long*, so that when the patron no longer wishes to hear or tolerate the pastor, he must leave and wander to some other place? then I answer: We are servants of God and this office is God's, to which we are called by God, albeit through men; this holy work must therefore be handled in a sacred way, but not according to human arbitrariness. **A shepherd and cowherd people may hire for a time, and when their service no longer pleases, they may at a definite time, but not always, dismiss them, if they wish: but so to treat a shepherd of souls is not within the power of any man. Nor may the servant of the Word himself accept the holy office in such a way, unless he wants to become a hireling.** Certainly those who would be thus called would not fulfill the office diligently and faithfully, but would become flatterers and say which pleases people, or they must constantly expect their service to be terminated" *(Pastorale evang.*, 104)...

J. P. Beyer, *"Vom Beruf zum Amt der Kirchendiener,"* LC-MS Eastern District *Proceedings*, (1889) 36-37.

This temporary calling is a shameful perversion of the order which Christ Himself has created in the church. Nowhere is it revealed as the will of God that preachers and teachers should be so engaged that it depends on the good will and the decision of the others whether they may remain in their office or not. In the most ancient church one therefore finds not a trace of such temporary employment. This vice arose only at the time of the Reformation, when some congregations misused the doctrine of the spiritual priesthood. [Luther strongly objected]. . .

As a result of this decided opposition to the excesses of congregations, we hear no more of such attempts in the Lutheran church for a long time.

Only at the time of the Interim, 1547--52, several south-German imperial cities began again to call their preachers for a certain number of years, and retained the contract system, even though the emergency was ended by the Passau Treaty in 1552. An Opinion of the Wittenberg Faculty in respect of a school-cantor, from the year 1638, reads: "The calls to church and schools services, in which one is to give the other Where there is a will to follow proper churchly practice, there will always be a way. The proposed document's treatment of the new concept of "intentional interim ministry" (see 40-41) does not face up sufficiently to the underlying issues of principle. Nor do the issues of "Resignation and Retirement" (45-46) appear to have been sufficiently thought through.

"A quarter year's notice without any other weighty cause, are entirely disapproved in our Lutheran churches" (*Consil. theol. Witeb* III, 55). . . As a result of such forceful testimonies against it, the temporary call disappeared again from Germany, but arose again about 200 years later in America. But also here the Saxons, who had immigrated 50 years ago, raised their voice against it, and showed the limits of congregational rights in call-matters, and maintained what we still teach today: A congregation has no right to call or dismiss a preacher or teacher by contract.

P. F. Koehneke, "The Call into the Holy Ministry," in *The Abiding Word* (St. Louis: Concordia Publishing House, 1946) 1:380.

From the beginning our Synod had to take a definite stand on this question. Among the conditions of membership in Synod the following is listed [in the Constitution]: **"Regular (not temporary) call of the pastor."** Chapter V, paragraph 11, we find this statement: "Licenses to preach which are customary in this country are not granted by Synod because they are contrary to Scripture and the practice of the Church". . . This has been the consistent practice of our Synod since that time and has been stated again and again in official papers presented at conventions and in our periodicals.

Robert D. Preus, "The Doctrine of the Call in the Confessions and Lutheran Orthodoxy," in *Church and Ministry Today*, ed. John A. Maxfield (Crestwood, Mo.: Luther Academy, 2001), 33.

The call is always permanent. The notion of a temporary call is inconceivable in the nature of the case, and therefore the matter is not even considered by Luther or the Confessions or any Lutheran theologian. The function of the ministerial office, Calov asserts, is to work for the church as a servant (*diaconus*), not as a lord, to do the work of an evangelist to the grave, to guard and be an example to the flock, an angel of God As revelation of His Word. One never quits such a calling. As the immediate call in apostolic times was for life (until God Himself called the person to a new place), so it is with the mediate call. **It is permanent and irrevocable, unless God Himself intervenes.**
Kurt Marquart
Walter Lehenbauer
April 29, 2003

CTCR INVITED TO RESPOND TO MARQUART-LEHENBAUER

July 14, 2003
To the CTCR
Fax (314) 996-1116
The July 21 CN will include the Marquart-Lehenbauer minority report.
CN will be glad to published any response CTCR staff members have to the minority report.
God's blessings,
Herman Otten

No Response

Christian News, July 21, 2003

1. "Ecumenical" and "ecumenism" come from the Greek word meaning ____.
2. The Lord makes His church ONE only in the ____.
3. There are true believers in all churches which ____.
4. The three basic versions of Christianity are ____.
5. What has the modern "Ecumenical Movement" given up? ____.
6. The bureaucries and seminaries of the "mainline" churches have ____.
7. Everywhere the sheep of Christ hunger for ____.
8. What did The Lutheran Church-Missouri Synod formerly say about a "temporary call?" ____.
9. Serious theology must contsantly call the church's practice back to ____.
10. Unsound practice ultimately leads to ____.
11. The call is always ____.

THE GIFTS OF THE SPIRIT TODAY

**Second Essay, Lutheran Church of Australia General Synod,
Hersham, Victoria, October, 1972
By Kurt Marquart**

No serious Christian can be smug about spiritual life in general – and his own in particular. He will always pray and reach for more from the Source of Life, both for himself and for others. But neither will he be able to despair of the Church because of the offences which beset him within and without! The Church, the spotless Bride of Christ, cleansed by the water-with-word washing (Eph. 5:26), remains in this life an article of faith, not of sight.

Some constructive dissatisfaction then is quite healthy. But it becomes counter-productive beyond certain limits. When, as happens today, the most basic Christian certainties are open to question, and doctrine, sacraments, Christian morality, even Christ Himself may be sacrificed on the altar of "Relevance", then the very basis for helpful change is lost. As Chesterton quipped, people who are forever changing their views about heaven will never be able to make the necessary changes on earth! And as reformation gives way to revolution and anarchy, there is an increasingly desperate clutching at straws.

One approach receiving wide acclaim today is neo-Pentecostalism or, more elegantly, the Charismatic Movement or Revival. This is supposed to solve the major problems of the modern Church. It is in terms of the crucial issues raised by this movement that I propose to deal with my assigned topic. My approach and analysis are heavily indebted to Frederick Bruner's *A Theology of the Holy Spirit* (London: Hodder and Stoughton, 1970), which I regard as the definitive work on the subject to date. But not all my conclusions should be blamed on Bruner.

To get hold of our subject clearly and precisely, let us look at it under two heads, **Ends** (i.e. goals, ideals, the desired "what" of spiritual gifts) and **Means** (the "how").

I. ENDS

A. Lists of the Gifts

Pentecostalism tends to think of the gifts of the Spirit as if they were standard, invariable functions, nine in number. The New Testament knows of no such standard list. The following texts (TEV) may reflect differing local conditions:

Rom. 12:5-8: "We are one body in union with Christ and we are all joined to each other as different parts of one body. So we are to use our different gifts in accordance with the grace that God has given us. If our gift is to preach God's message ('prophecy'), we must do it according to the faith ... If it is to serve, we must serve. If it is to teach, we must teach. If it is to encourage others, we must do so. Whoever shares what he has with others, must do it generously; whoever has authority, must work hard;

whoever shows kindness to others, must do it cheerfully."

I Cor. 12:4-11: "There are different kinds of spiritual gifts ('charismata'), but the same Spirit saves them. There are different ways of serving, but the same Lord is served. There are different abilities to perform service, but the same God gives ability to everyone for all services. Each one is given some proof of the Spirit's presence for the good of all. The Spirit gives one man a message of wisdom while to another man the same Spirit gives a message of knowledge. One and the same Spirit gives faith to one man, while to another man he gives the power to heal. The Spirit gives one man the power to work miracles; to another the gift of preaching God's message ('prophecy'); and to yet another, the ability to tell the difference between gifts that come from the Spirit and those that do not. To one man he gives the ability to speak with strange sounds; to another he gives the ability to explain what these sounds mean. But it is one and the same Spirit who does all this; he gives a different gift to each man, as he wishes."

I Cor. 12:28-31: "In the church, then, God has put all in place: in the first place, apostles, in the second place, prophets, and in the third place, teachers; then those who perform miracles, followed by those who are given the power to heal, or to help others, or to direct them, or to speak with strange sounds. They are not all apostles, or prophets, or teachers. Not all have the power to work miracles or to heal diseases, or to speak with strange sounds, or to explain what these sounds mean. Set your hearts, then, on the more important gifts."

Eph. 4:11-12: "It was he who 'gave gifts to men'; he appointed some to be apostles, others to be prophets, others to be evangelists, others to be pastors and teachers. He did this to prepare all God's people for the work of Christian service, to build up the body of Christ."

I Peter 4:10-11: "Each one, as a good manager of God's different gifts, must use for the good of others the special gift he has received from God. Whoever preaches, must preach God's words; whoever serves, must serve with the strength that God gives him."

B. General Comments

1. "Prominent at the head are gifts of intelligent and thoughtful utterance. Prominent at the end are gifts of ecstatic utterance". (1)

Note the same scale of values in I Tim. 5:17: "worthy of double honour, especially those who labour in preaching and teaching".

2. As their very name (**charisma**, free gift, favour) indicates, the Spirit's gifts are not religious achievements, or marks of special holiness (as Pentecostalism tends to see them), but free gifts of grace (**charis**), given by the Spirit as he wishes (I Cor. 12: 11).

3. The whole point of the gifts is missed if they are used, as in Pentecostalism, to divide Christians into "higher" (charismatic) and "lower" (nominal Christians; those who have received only "water baptism", but not "Spirit Baptism") types. The One Spirit creates and animates One Body (Eph. 4:1-16) and any distinction between "first class" and "economy class" Christians is intolerable (Gal. 2:11-21; Eph. 2:11-22). Bruner: "It

was to avoid, not to introduce, such divisions that Paul wrote I Corinthians 12:13". (2)

4. The chapter on love, sandwiched between I Cor. 12 and 14, is needed to see spiritual gifts in their true light. However great the glory of the gifts, love is "a still more excellent way" (12:31). "So faith, hope, love abide, these three; but the greatest of these is love" (13:13). Indeed, wherever the gifts are listed, love figures prominently in the context, e.g. Rom. 12:9.10 to 13:8-10; I Cor. 13; Eph. 3:17-19; 4:2, 5.16; I Peter4:8)!

Love is the first and noblest fruit of the Spirit, Gal. 5:22:23: "love, joy, peace, patience, kindness, goodness, trustfulness (or faithfulness), gentleness and self-control." This is permanent, constant, and indicative of real maturity always and everywhere. This is not true of the "service gifts" (I Cor. 13:1-3). The Corinthians evidently overvalued these special gifts, particularly tongues, and undervalued love.

5. Love (**agape**) is not a passion, but a sober ethical principle. This sobriety, as opposed to religious emotionalism, is Paul's concern at the very beginning of his discussion of spiritual gifts (12:2):

> The very characteristic of the Corinthians' heathen past, he argues, was the sense of being overpowered and carried away by spiritual forces.
>
> You know how, in the days when you were still pagan, you were swept off to those dumb heathen gods, however you happened to be led (I Cor. 12:2 NEB; margin; 'you would be seized by some power which drove you to those dumb heathen gods']. 'There is no doubt at all', Schrenk comments, 'that Paul intends to say here,' The truly spiritual is not marked by a being swept away (**Hingerissenwerden**); that was precisely the characteristic of your previous fanatical religion." It is important to notice that Paul places this valuation of the spiritually 'sweeping' at the very outset of his treatment of 'spiritual things' in Corinth. As the superscripture to his essay in chapters twelve to fourteen Paul has written: Seizure is not necessarily Christian or paramountly spiritual. The relevance to Pentecostalism does not need to be stressed. (3)

The relevance to liturgical experimentation, however, may need to be stressed: its inspiration and control must be Christian sobriety, not the orgiastic pagan frenzy of drug-and-pop festivals (Eph.5: 18-20)!

C. The Gifts in Detail

In order to visualize concrete modern versions and applications of the spiritual gifts in the New Testament, let us look at some in detail:

> What is the difference between the **"teaching"** and the **"encouraging"** of Rom. 12:7? Perhaps, as Luther thought, the former referred to the instruction of people being won for the Faith, while the latter meant helping believers to grow in grace. It is obvious that pastors today need both gifts. But not only they. Christians in all walks of life have opportunities to draw people to Christ, or to encourage believers toward a deeper participation in the divine life. The gifts should also be used for various special ministries, like

teaching (full-time, part-time, R.I., Sunday schools), counseling, youth work, elders' work, deaconess' work, and apologetic—missionary work in universities and other centres of learning, and in the community generally.

Another difficult distinction is between the **"utterance of wisdom"** and the **"utterance of knowledge"** in I Cor. 12:8. The Jerusalem Bible says of the first: "Probably the gift of preaching the central Christian truths about God and God's life in us: this is the 'perfect teaching' of Heb. 6:1. Cf. also I Cor. 2:6-16"; and of the second: "The gift of preaching the elementary Christian truths: 'the elementary teaching concerning Christ' of Heb. 6:1".

But others have held that **"wisdom"** refers more to the practical application of Christian truth to daily life, while **"knowledge"** implies a deeper, even mystical, insight into the real nature of God and of divine life. Pastors and teachers, and those who train and lead them, are by virtue of their office in need of these gifts.

The **"evangelists"** of Eph. 4:11 appear to have been people who had memorized reliable accounts or summaries of the evangel, the Good News of the life, death, and resurrection of Jesus Christ, and could recite and report these facts as the occasion demanded. No doubt it was writings based on such reports which the Evangelist St. Luke carefully sifted in the course of his own work (St. Luke 1:1-4). Such oral reports would, with the passage of time, have become increasingly unreliable, hence the authentic apostolic message had to be fixed in writing for all time: "These have been written that you may believe that Jesus is the Messiah, the Son of God, and that through this faith you may have life in his name" (John 20:31).

The ability to understand and explain the written apostolic Gospels in an accurate and relevant way, seeing the details in terms of the main thrusts, would be today's equivalent of the special grace of being an "evangelist".

The **"serving"** of Rom. 12:7 is given as "administration" in the Jerusalem Bible, and in v. 8 the "officials" are told to be "diligent". The former probably are the congregation's active workers or office-bearers generally, while the latter would be the actual leaders. The gift of leading without exploiting, manipulating, or putting on airs –so foreign to the world's "chain of command" notions (Matt. 20:25-28), and so deflating to all puffed-up bubbles of vanity over the "status" of pastor, lecturer, chairman, elder, or treasurer's cousin! – is a precious blessing in the Church.

"Sharing" (Rom. 12:8), whether of bodily or spiritual goods, is to be done with "simplicity", that is, with single-minded devotion to God, without worrying about recognition, "fair shares", human "deserving", and the like. If this dangerous gift became wide-spread, the Church would face the problem of how to dispose of all its surplus talents and funds, instead of having to juggle man-power and budget figures to make ends meet. But of course the gift refers not primarily to money, but to that complete sharing, in the family context of the congregation, to which the early Church was accustomed (Acts 2:44-46). Today the gift could be exercised in any number of ways, e.g. singing in the choir, taking people who are without transport to and from church and meetings, sending congratulation cards to the parents of babies just baptized, supporting the work with money, organizing Bible classes, adopting orphaned children within the congregation, etc. The emphasis is on the church as family, sharing each other's joys and sorrows, sticking together for the common work.

Doing **"works of mercy"** or showing "kindness to others" (v.8), is much more specifically pointed toward unfortunate and underprivileged people of all kinds, and not necessarily within the Church. This is person-to-person help —not a cold, anonymous two-bob-to-a-door-knock-appeal thing — and it must be offered not grudgingly or perfunctorily or condescendingly, but "cheerfully", with obvious joy and gladness, for God loves a cheerful giver (II Cor. 9:7). St. John Chrysostom explains the need for cheerfulness: "Nothing seems so humiliating to a man as to have to receive from others: if you do not by means of the greatest gladness dispel the suspicion and show that you are receiving more than you give, you do more to cast the recipient down than to lift him up"!

This is not to deny the necessity, in our type of society, of exercising this gift also through humanitarian organizations. But the gift will never be without personal concern and involvement.

In our world of suffering Christians and suffering humanity there is much need and scope for the Christ-like gift of compassion. One caution, however: If the entire budget of the L.C.A. were devoted to world relief, (a) it wouldn't make a dent in human misery globally, but (b) the L.C.A. would be minus its overseas and Aboriginal missions, seminary, and schools! The early Church avoided this sort of dilemma: apart from the individual Christians' personal generosity wherever they were, the organized Church did not undertake any responsibility to provide for the physical needs of all unfortunates in the Roman Empire, or even in Jerusalem, but took up special offerings for fellow-Christians in special emergencies, e.g. the oppressed "saints" in Jerusalem (I Cor. 16:1-3)!

Summing up, the main gifts of the Spirit amount to this, that the life-giving Gospel is effectively implemented, i.e. "speaking the truth in love, we are to grow up in every way into him who is the head, into Christ" (Eph. 4: 15 R.S.V.), so that "the whole body grows and builds itself up through love" (v.16 T.E.V.). If this is happening, the Church has all she needs for her life and health. If it isn't, all talk about "gifts of the Spirit" is hot air.

D. The Pentecostal " Specials"

Pentecostalism's peculiar stress is not on the quiet, "ordinary" gifts, but on the dramatic, obviously miraculous ones: tongues, healing, prophecy. These are emphasized out of all proportion.

Tongues: Pentecostalism distinguishes between the purposes of tongues in Acts and those in Corinth. The Acts tongues are supposed to happen to a person only once, at this "Baptism in the Holy Spirit". In this scheme a person is first born again by faith, has his sins forgiven, and receives the sign of "water baptism". Then, after a longer or shorter period of "tarrying", praying, "yielding", and reaching the necessary level of obedience, he ought to receive "Spirit Baptism", which is an emotional experience marked by ecstatic speech, i.e. tongues. This is now the signal or proof that he has received the Spirit's fulness, and with it come Spirit-gifts for effective service. One of these, again, is tongues, but this time the "Corinthian" kind, which can be used more or less at will, while the once-only "Acts" kind is involuntary.

That the gift of tongues could exist today few would deny. Even Dr. Kurt Koch, who is very critical of Pentecostalism in his **The Strife of Tongues**, refers to some cases which struck him as genuine. John Sherrill, the Pentecostal author of the persuasive and attractively written book **They Speak with Other Tongues**, gives cases which, if accurately reported, strike me as genuine sparks of the real Pentecost. For instance, an American missionary in Africa, H.B. Garlock, having been captured in 1922 by a savage cannibal tribe, the Pahns, gathered from the witch-Doctor's menacing tone and gestures that he was to be done to death. He shook violently, prayed, and then –

> Garlock felt a strange boldness. He took a deep breath and began to speak. From his lips came a flow of words which he did not understand. Garlock saw the natives lean forward, enthralled. He saw that the words – whatever they were – had a stirring effect on those who listened. He knew beyond a doubt that he was speaking to the Pahns in their own language. For twenty minutes Garlock talked to the Pahns. Then, as suddenly as the speech-power came, it vanished. (4)

The upshot of it was that Garlock was released and the Pahns eventually accepted Christianity. If correctly reported, we have here a real miracle of God.

But such unusual cases do not represent the run-of-the-mill Pentecostal experience, and do not prove the latter genuine. There are several alternatives. First, tongues can be demonic. Far from being distinctively Christian, ecstatic speech is quite typical of many pagan religions. Sherrill himself reports that in 1855 the Mormons in Nauvoo, Illinois, were speaking in tongues, and that the 7th article of their creed explicitly teaches this practice. (5) And no informed person can possibly identify the crude gods of Mormonism with the Holy Trinity. Thus early Mormonism's practice, which Sherrill seems to accept as quite the same sort of thing as Pentecostalism's, could not possibly have been a gift of the Holy Spirit! Indeed, Dr. Koch traces a connection between Pentecostal "tongues" and spiritism! And such "tongues" have been known not only to deceive, but to blaspheme the Name of Jesus!

Secondly, linguistic analysis of typical "tongues" shows that they do not resemble known languages in structure. They are more like sonic debris or "decayed speech", and the "interpretations" seem to bear no relation to the sound sequences of the "tongues", or even their length. The "interpretations" are usually hackneyed strings of King James Version verbiage, of no obvious significance or importance. Some studies also suggest that the ecstatic speech of "tongues" may be a form of psychological abnormality.

Two brief and popular treatments of the subject are Donald W. Burdick, **Tongues: To Speak Or Not To Speak** (Chicago: Moody Press, 1970) and Professor Anthony A. Hoekema, **What About Tongue-Speaking?** (Exeter: Paternoster Press, 1966).

If anyone has a genuine gift of tongues, it must be used in the modest, balanced manner St. Paul presribes, and that would create no problem. Nor does the absence of this gift create a problem - faith, hope, and love are the important things. What creates the problem is the Pentecostal claim that "speaking in tongues" is an important, even the important test of spiritual blessing and fullness!

Healing: Again, that remarkable cures occur cannot be doubted. Dr. Kurt Koch himself has written a most enthusiastic account of **The Revival in Indonesia**, in which he refers to tens of thousands of healings, and quite apart from any Pentecostalism!

Evil, demonic forces can of course also heal and work miracles, in the interests of false gospels like the Marian cults of Lourdes and Fatima, the escapist delusions of "Christian Science", or the spiritist séance craze (cf. II Thess. 2:9-12). Plain fraud and humbug too are not unknown among Pentecostal healings! (6)

And then there are people – from time to time reported in the press – who just have a natural "knack" for healing, usually by the laying on of hands, but without Christian or religious connections of any kind. Genuine, Spirit-given healing, we may be sure, will never foster personality cults, nor feed the anti-Christian delusion that if only faith is strong enough, all disease must be cured. On the contrary, Christian faith submits humbly and trustingly, even in great suffering (II Cor. 12:7-to), to the will of Him who knows and loves best, whose "caresses leave wounds" (Ibsen's **Brand**).

A former healer in China, Mr. Ching, has said:

> The further one travels on the way of life, and the nearer one approaches Him who is Life, the more one knows that miracles and outward manifestations are dangerous. Enter into the heart of our Lord's suffering. The way there is not the way of freedom from bodily infirmity and pain. (7) Dr. D.V. Rees, who reports this, experienced the truth of it himself:

> Two of our children died of measles during the great measles epidemic which struck North China. I was standing beside the cot of one of these little ones, while it was in extremis. We had done all we could. Mr. Ching came and stood beside me and began to pray for the child. "Now", I thought, "we will see a miracle." For Mr. Ching's early ministry had been born in miracle. But as he was praying the little one died.

> When he heard that its breathing had ceased, he put his hand on my shoulder, and said, "Dear brother, three or four years ago that wouldn't have happened to me. If I had prayed for that child then, it would have lived. But things have changed since then and I would not have it otherwise. Do you know that power can be a dangerous thing, even power from God? It can fill one with spiritual pride. It is not power

96

that I choose but a deeper death. Oh, that the power of Calvary might be seen in me!"

That night he preached to about a thousand Christian Chinese on such Biblical characters as Balaam, Samson, and Saul, the king of Israel. "Were their lives in keeping with the power they had?" (8)

Prophecy: Pentecostalism understands prophecy, like "tongues", as ecstatic or semi-ecstatic speech, but in a known language, and conveying direct messages or revelations from the Spirit. Luther, on the other hand, says that the "noblest, highest and greatest gift of prophecy" is the right explanation and interpretation of Scripture.

At first sight it appears as if Pentecostalism fits the New Testament data better than does Luther. The Jerusalem Bible comments on Acts 11:27 that the prophets do not simply foretell the future, Acts 11:28; 21:11, or read hearts, I Cor.14:24-25; cf. I Tim. 1:18. When they 'edify, exhort, console', I Cor. 14:3; cf. Acts 4:36; 11:23-24, they do so by a supernatural revelation; in this they resemble those who 'speak strange languages', Acts 2:4; 19:6, but their gift is greater because their speech is intelligible, I Cor. 14. Their chief work was evidently to explain the oracles of Scripture under the guidance of the Holy Spirit, especially those of the O.T. prophets, I Peter 1:10-12, and thus expound the 'mystery' of the divine plan, I Cor. 13:2; Eph. 3:5; Rom. 16:25. For this reason they are named with the apostles as the foundation of the Church, Eph. 2:20. The Revelation of St. John is a typical example of this N.T. 'prophecy', Rev. l:3 ...

This suggests that Luther got hold of the permanent **essence** or **content** of prophecy (seeing the mystery of God's Gift in His Son as the core, key, and theme of Scripture), while Pentecostalism clings to the temporary outward form, the outworn empty shell of ecstatic speech! For the joint reference to the "apostles and prophets" as together constituting the "foundation" of the Church (Eph. 2:20) suggests that prophets, like the apostles, were a temporary institution, not a permanent office. And if we imagine the difficulty of establishing and developing congregations without a written New Testament, we can guess why "prophets" were needed: to provide the Church in its formative years with reliable guidance in the understanding of Scripture-fulfilled-in-Christ and its application to all sorts of perplexing situations. The Apostles could not be personally present everywhere – nor could their unique office (Acts 1:21-22) be "inflated" into a membership of hundreds, scattered here, there, and everywhere! So, until the Apostles' and their chosen assistants' inspired writings –if even all Old Testament Scripture was God-inspired, 2 Tim. 3:16, how much more the documents issuing from the very fullness of Pentecost itself! – were composed and became available to congregations everywhere, the prophets had to fill the gap. And if this was their function, it makes good sense that they are listed as coming "second", right after the Apostles (I Cor: 12:28). Even so, the original kind of prophecy may still occur in unusual missionary situations - for instance in Indonesia. It seems that the Christians of Timor were warned, by prophecy, again at some Pentecostal tongue-mongers who were about to arrive from overseas! (9).

Naturally prophecy, like the other gifts, must be tested by apostolic truth. It must be according to the analogy or proportion of the Faith (Rom. 12: 16).

Today it is a matter of seeing the relevance of Apostolic teaching to our own circumstances. Berkhof's opinion that "prophecy is the gift of understanding and expressing what the will of God is for a given present situation" (10) is illuminating, for real teaching and preaching is not of course a matter of parroting set slogans. Every long-suffering hearer in the pew who has ever been subjected to orthodox but "unrelevanted", unapplied strings of Bible texts doctrinal formulas, and insipidly generalized exhortations, will appreciate how important for the Church is the gift of coming to grips, Biblically, with concrete here-and-now human realities.

E. The Point: Building Up the Body

Paul's accomplishment in these three chapters is to have impressed upon the faith of the Corinthians that as the Spirit is united to Christ so the varied gifts of the Spirit are committed to the up building of the body of Christ. The triune God is the source, love is the way, and the upbuilding of the church is the goal of the spiritual graces.

The impact of this three-chapter tract must be such as to make it difficult for any church to find the essence of the spiritual in the merely enthusiastic or the only visibly miraculous. One must have the impression instead that, according to Paul, the Christian spiritual is that which confesses the deity of Jesus by faith and which thus works through intelligent love for the up building of Christ's body the church. (11)

This upbuilding involves two aspects, the apostolic mission of evangelizing all nations (Matt. 28:19), and the spiritual cultivation - for service - of those in the Church.

When one thinks of people like David Wilkerson, of Cross and Switchblade fame, one cannot but be deeply impressed by the resolute zeal of his kind of Pentecostal mission work. Other Christians - except the Salvation Army it seems - have too often identified Christian life with rigorous middle-class respectability, without any effort to reach out to "no-hoper" types of the lower and "social problem" strata of society. This must be said to our shame. But Pentecostal mission effort has yet another strength. Despite its specific fallacies, it is based on a clear-cut, no-nonsense approach to the realities of sin and grace. These people call a spade a spade, without hemming and hawing, without letting every Biblical affirmation die the death of a thousand embarrassed qualifications! How different from a certain type of worldly-wise, Sadducean, "Ecumenical" churchmanship, which has given up on the supernatural, and acts as "a churchy sort of U.N." in trying to save the world secularly. It even attacks the churches for having in the past more often "conceived their task as one of 'bringing Christ to the nations' than as witness to the Christ who is already present in the processes of life and death"! (12) No mission work is possible on that basis. The Pentecostals, despite their faults, are at least quite clear about the fact that the Word of Christ needs to be brought to people, since

Christ is NOT "already present in the processes of life and death" under paganism. The "Jesus Revolution" is a crying out of stones - because so much of churchianity is silent or mumbling to itself!

We pastors particularly, as the successors of the Apostles in the Public Ministry, must see our chief task as one of pressing the claims of Christ, not just privately or in the semi-secrecy of our churches, but in public; and of helping God's people whom we serve to shape themselves into congregations that are effective instruments of outreach. To this end our schedules must be cleared, where necessary, of deacons' work (Acts 6:2) - not to mention plain trivia. But there is a dark side to Pentecostal mission work. Bruner reports a big occasion in which a local high school choir had been asked to participate. As things got really "Pentecostal", the students "began gradually to leave the large hall until almost all of them had gone . . . Many are turned away from the Christian faith by the irrational Pentecostal manifestation of it. I affirm this in the face of Pentecostalism's advertisement of its missionary successes. Unfortunately, those who are driven out cannot always, like those who come in, be counted." (13)

The great fault of Pentecostal mission work is that it often tends to be parasitic, to draw crowds from other churches rather than from the unchurched and the pagans. In Indonesia the great spiritual revival originated generally outside the Pentecostal movement, though the latter tried, with little success, to infiltrate and exploit the revival in the interests of the tongues-excitement. (14)

When it comes to the second great aspect of the up building of the Body, we have perhaps even more to learn from the Pentecostals. At a time when some are openly advocating the complete abandonment of organized parish life as stale and irrelevant, Pentecostalism can extract this tribute from Bruner: "AS IN THE NEW TESTAMENT, THE CONGREGATIONAL FELLOWSHIP OF BELIEVERS IS EXPERIENCED AS NOTHING LESS SIGNIFICANT THAN THE CENTRE OF THE CHRISTIAN LIFE" (15). Enthusiastic, active participation by the whole priesthood of believers; an all-pervading sense of joy; and a sense of the closeness of the power and majesty of God; these are indeed the features of New Testament worship. Where this is lacking, and the "worship service" is experienced as a one-man show or as dead-weight and drudgery, the problem is not solved but hidden by escaping into auxiliaries, Sunday School, etc. These are very useful on the periphery, but cannot take the place of the centre!

Indeed, "the congregation's active sharing of ministry is the most impressive lesson for the historic churches from I Cor. 14 - and from Pentecostalism". (16)

II. MEANS

A. The Full Gospel

(1) The Gospel as life-power: As God gives Himself only in Christ, and that fully, so Christ gives Himself only in the Gospel - and that fully! The whole point of Christianity is that God's life is in the Son (I John 5: 11), apart from Whom there is no access to the Father (John 14:6) so that "whoever has the Son has this life; whoever does not have the Son of God does not have life" (I John 5: 12). And all this is said precisely of the concrete historical swaddling-clothed-crucified-risen Person of Jesus. For it is the Word-made-flesh Who is "full of grace and truth" (John 1:14), and it is this flesh which is the Bread of Life, given for the salvation of the world (John 6:51). As Luther comments on Col. 2:9: "So it is final, says St. Paul, the whole, total Godhead dwells bodily, that is personally, in Jesus Christ. Therefore the fellow who does not find or get God in Christ shall never again and nowhere else have or find God outside of Christ, even if he goes, as it were, over heaven, under hell, or into space." (17)

It is this very heart of Biblical Christianity which Pentecostalism violates by pretending that there is something more, something above and beyond the "mere Christianity" of believing in Christ, being reborn, and having one's sins forgiven. Beyond this incomplete, preparatory stage there is still the "fullness of the Spirit" and of His gifts, to be obtained in a second and separate work, the "Baptism in the Spirit", of which speaking in tongues is the outward proof! But this concept of the incompleteness of a "mere" life in Christ, needing to be supplemented by the Spirit, is intolerable. (For a documentation of the fairness of this description see the copious quotations from leading Pentecostal writers in Bruner's book). We have here precisely the Colossian heresy against which Paul wrote: "IN HIM ALL THE FULNESS OF GOD'S VERY BEING DWELLS BODILY, AND YOU ARE COMPLETELY FULFILLED IN HIM" (Col. 2:9). And what are poor miserable tongues, even if genuine, compared to the glory of Christ living in us, so that having our "roots and foundations in love", we may know the vast dimensions of Christ's love, "and so be completely filled with the perfect fullness of God" (Eph. 3:17-19)? It is Christ Who has the Spirit "not by measure" (John 3:34) but totally. To suggest therefore that there is any sort of fuller fullness, anything at all still lacking and incomplete in "mere" life in Christ, so that we need not merely constant growth in the fullness of Christ but something new and different over and above this, is not a "full" Gospel, but "another gospel", though there can be no other (Gal. 1:6.7). It is blasphemy.

The New Testament teaches further that the fullness that is in Christ is offered and imparted to us only in the Gospel, but there fully. The seed of spiritual life is the Word of God (Luke 8: 11). Christ's words are spirit and life (John 6:63). Hence his Gospel is not mere information, a dead letter needing life from elsewhere, it is not an empty sign which happens to accompany a Spirit-action independent of it, but it is the power (dynamis) of God for salvation(Rom. 1:16), creating faith (Rom. 10:17), and thus begetting Christians (I Cor. 4:15), so that we are saved by the Gospel (I Cor. 15:l)! And this Gospel in a nutshell is the Absolution (John 20:23).

In place of this really full Gospel, Pentecostalism comes with its doctrine of conditions: to advance from ordinary Christian faith to "Spirit-fulness" it is necessary to pray, wrestle, conquer sin, "yield", and "tarry", so that when the necessary level of obedience and holiness is reached, God may grant the "Baptism in the Spirit", with tongues and the other gifts. This is exactly the Galatian heresy, met head-on by St. Paul:

100

You foolish Galatians! Who put a spell on you? Right before your eyes you had a plain description of the death of Jesus Christ on the cross! Tell me just this one thing: did you receive God's Spirit by doing what the Law requires, or by hearing and believing the gospel? How can you be so foolish! You began by God's Spirit; do you now want to finish by your own power? . ... When God gives you the Spirit and works miracles among you, does he do it because you do what the Law requires, or because you hear and believe the gospel? (Gal. 3: 1-5)

"As in Galatia", comments Bruner, "the Pentecostal peril consists in seeking spiritual fullness through fulfilling of special conditions rather than as in the beginning, through the message of faith alone apart from all conditions." (18) And the "message of faith", the Gospel, is called "the service of the Spirit" not in the sense of tongues, etc., but because of its real glory of being "the service of righteousness", i.e. JUSTIFICATION, FORGIVENESS (II Cor. 3:9)!

Beyond the one Spirit-filled Gospel of Christ there is nothing more, no "second blessing". The Sacraments are not additions to the Gospel, but the same Gospel in action. Baptism is a water-with-the-word washing (Eph. 5: 26) and the Eucharist offers the very Blood of the New Covenant (Matt. 26:28). The God-in-Christ and Christ-in-the-Gospel themes come together in the depth and simplicity of I John 5:6-8:

HE CAME [past tense - THEN] NOT ONLY WITH THE WATER, BUT WITH BOTH THE WATER AND THE BLOOD . ... THERE ARE [present tense - NOW] THREE WITNESSES, THE SPIRIT, THE WATER, AND THE BLOOD; AND ALL THREE AGREE.

This high, "incarnational" doctrine of the full Gospel, including the Sacraments, needs to be stressed in our preaching and Church life. We cannot, for instance, be content with the general approach of "evangelical Protestantism" in Bible study and Sunday school materials. Apart from the typical moralism, which as one serious Calvinist bitterly complained, is "subversive of all Christianity", (19) general Protestant interpretation stops with the "then" of Jesus. We must move on to the "now" of preaching and the Sacraments. For example, the Ark of Noah must be seen not only as a deliverance from judgment, pointing to Christ, but as a picture of our own Baptism, which now really ("antitypically") saves us (I Peter 3:21). The Passover must be understood as prefiguring not only the crucified Lamb of God then, but also our Liturgy today, in which He now feeds us with His body and blood. Scripture interpretation must not come to rest in mere reminders and meanings of what happened THEN in the first century, but must effectively continue all the fullness of the THEN into the NOW of our Baptism, preaching, and Eucharist!

(2) The Gospel as doctrine: In a sense the Pentecostal mini-gospel about tongues is simply a religious expression of the mood and spirit of the times. Let me explain.

In two fascinating books, **The God Who is There** and **Escape From Reason,** Francis Schaeffer argues that modern man has given up on reason, and is trying to find meaning and purpose in unreason - in poetry, music, art, mysticism, drugs, sex, power, and so on. Why? When our Western thinkers abandoned God for all practical purposes, they were convinced that human reason could go it alone, and could by itself, without divine revelation, find out all it needed to know about the universe and man's place in it. But reason over-reached itself and suffered a hernia: having questioned everything else, it finally questioned itself.

Now, if there is no God, no creative Mind behind the universe, if it is all one big accident, then man is simply part of that accident and his life means nothing. Everything is a pointless jumble of atoms and molecules, and any ideas of mind, soul, conscience, and morality are just illusions. Man is a product of chance, a bundle of biochemically determined instincts, like a rat, and no more. It follows of course that the universe has no objective meaning, and that everybody must therefore create his own meaning, that is, he must play God. In such a scheme nothing can be "right" or "wrong", but everything is a matter of taste: some people like abortion and sodomy, and others don't - exactly as some people like spinach and others hate it!

This suicide of thought robbed of meaning ("their thoughts have become complete nonsense and their empty minds are filled with darkness", Rom. 1!), says Schaeffer, has infected our whole culture, being spread among the masses precisely by "good" cinema: The basic message of Antonioni's famous film "Blow-Up" was captured in the ads: "Murder without guilt. Love without meaning."

Modern "theology", like a Johnny-come-lately, has picked up the prevailing mood, and drawn the appropriate conclusions for religion: There is no objective truth in the sense of doctrine or statements; truth is subjective and happens in "encounter" or experience, whatever that may mean. The Ten Commandments become Ten Suggestions, and enter the New Morality. Revelation is out, and Revolution in!

This theological crisis affects far more than a few radical extremists. Harry Blamires, in his book **The Christian Mind**, says that "the Church" is content to cultivate the will and the feelings in private piety and morality, but has surrendered the mind unconditionally to secularism. The modern Christian is not expected to think Christianly, but to take over ready-made the secularist world-view presided over by secular universities. And so, wrote Malcolm Muggeridge somewhere, "The Bishops, though socially still very much in evidence, are intellectually in hiding"!

That is deeply tragic, because it is a bishop's (i.e. pastor's) first and foremost duty to teach. And there is in today's chaos a vast hunger for answers, for sense, meaning, and purpose. Why if not from a most desperate thirst for explanations, would anybody bother about absurdities like **Chariots of the Gods?** Or worse, as Whitaker Chambers wrote: "Communists are that part of mankind which has recovered the power to live or die - to bear witness - for its faith." (20)

Man is not an overgrown rat, and he must have meaning or die. Now, Christ is God's Word (Logos, John 1:1), the divine Reason, Plan, and Meaning of the universe. He is God's Message, and His Gospel is not irrational gibberish or airy-fairy waffling (I Cor. 14:7 ff.), but sober truth about solid acts and facts and their meanings. The Lordship of Christ is not only for the heart, but also for the head, for the intellect (II Cor. 10:5). And just because it is doctrinal substance, not formal verbal incantations, the Gospel cannot be "forced up once and for all" with a few easy formulas and slogans, so that we can "get on with the real work". Faithfulness to the Gospel requires not just the right phrases in constitutions - that can be the deadest of "dead orthodoxy" - but patient attention to the details of ever new issues, definitions, and confrontations. It means testing the spirits, constant decision-making, accepting this, rejecting that, in accordance with the doctrine of the Gospel "in all its articles" (Formula of Concord, Solid Declaration, X, 3lx). It involves intensive study, teaching - never were full time church schools and serious involvement in university work more vital than today! - publishing, discussing, debating (Acts 19:8-9), in short, strenuous spiritual-intellectual labour.

And what is Pentecostalism's distinctive contribution to these titanic needs and struggles within and without Christendom? Tongues! The false ecumenicity based on "tongues" pretends to heal the doctrinal divisions among Christians. Actually these divisions are simply ignored, since "dry", intellectual things like doctrines don't matter anyway. The result is that the "Lutheran" tongues-"charismatic" tends to feel closer to his Roman Catholic or Calvinist fellow-"charismatic", than to Lutherans without "tongues". This must mean that "tongues" are so important that by comparison differences over justification, the cult of Mary, Biblical vs. Papal authority, or the Sacramental Presence, matter little if at all. That certainly wasn't Paul's idea of the Gospel (Rom. 16: 17; Gal. 1:8.9), but it fits in perfectly with the anti-rational temper of the times.

Today's hunger for meaning must be met, and the spells of our secular witch-doctors broken, who ensnare our culture with the webs of false, deadly meanings. But this cannot be done with a soggy theology which avoids and evades real issues by escaping into irrational tongues! The power of truth, not of sound, must do it!

B. Baptism
The New Testament teaches only one Baptism (Eph. 4:5), which is neither a water-only nor a Spirit-only, but a water-and-Spirit Baptism (John 3:5). It is not a mere sign, picture, or expression, but an effective offer and application of Gospel power. As such it imparts not a preliminary ration, to be followed by more upon good behavior, but the whole Spirit-fullness of Christ. The very Pentecost promise is: "Repent and be **baptized** (water-baptism) . ... into the Name of Jesus Christ, into the **forgiveness of sins**, and you will receive the **gift of the Holy Spirit**" (Acts 2:38). (Note: Heb. 6:2 does not teach several baptisms, but shows the need to distinguish Christian Baptism from all sorts of religious washings practiced by Jews and pagans.) Accordingly, Baptism is said to "wash away" sins (Acts 22: 16), to "implant" in Christ's death and resurrection (Rom. 6:3-5), to be a "putting on" of Christ (Gal. 3:26-27). It is a "washing of water in the Word" (Eph. 5:26) and a "bath of rebirth and of the renewal of the Holy Spirit", through which God "saved" us (Tit. 3:5). We are buried and raised with

Christ by Baptism through faith (Col. 2:11). And again, Baptism actually "saves" (I Pet. 3:21).

Babies are not to be excluded from this gift, especially since (I) Christ welcomes children (Mark 10:14), but has established Baptism in His Church, and not child-blessing or "dedication" rites; and "the promise is to you and to your children" (Acts 2:39); (2) Babies too have spiritual needs (John 3:6; Eph. 2: 1.3); (3) The parallel of Circumcision, administered on the eighth day, suggests no age discrimination for the much greater gift of Baptism (Col. 2:9-13); and (4) Spiritual life, that is, faith, does not depend absolutely on conscious mental understanding and awareness - e.g. sleep, unconsciousness, insanity. Note also the extraordinary spiritual life of John the Baptist even before birth (Luke 1:15.44)!

But does not the Book of Acts establish the pattern: first water-baptism for the forgiveness of sins, and then later Spirit-baptism with the gift of tongues? No! The contrast between water-baptism and Spirit-baptism is not between Christian baptism and tongues, but between John's baptism and Pentecost (Acts 1:5). Out of this Pentecost-fullness issue Christian preaching and Baptism. Christian "water-baptism" therefore is Spirit-baptism, just as Peter says: "be baptised . .. into the forgiveness of sins, and you will receive the gift of the Holy Spirit" (2:38). The tongues of Pentecost (note that they were not gibberish but understandable languages, 2:8 ff.) were outward signs of the Spirit's fullness, but certainly not that fullness itself - other gifts are better and more vital, and love is the best of all, 1 Cor. 12-14! It is that real Spirit-fullness, not particular outward signs or phenomena, which Christian Baptism offers and imparts. Today there is no such thing as a pre-Pentecost baptism, and no "tarrying" in Jerusalem. There is only one post-Pentecost-fullness, offered in preaching and in the one Baptism!

Even in the Acts accounts there is no evidence that Christian converts generally received the Pentecost-tongues. Nothing is said about the 3000 converts of Pentecost itself receiving and tongues or other special signs beyond Baptism itself. Rather, miracles and signs happened "through the Apostles" (Acts 2:43). And it is probably the small group of Acts (1:13-14, not the whole 120, who would hardly have been in "one room" (2: 1), who spoke in tongues on Pentecost Day. The only other instances of Pentecost-like tongues occur at crucial new stages of the divinely given mission programme (Acts 1:8): stage two, Samaria (8:4-24), and stage three, "uttermost parts," first the Gentiles at Caesarea (10:44-46) and then the special situation in Ephesus (19:1-7).

The Ephesians' trouble was not that they had had only "water baptism" but that they had had only John's baptism. And that they hadn't heard "that there was a Holy Spirit" (19:2) means, comparing the wording with John 7:39, that they didn't know that the Spirit's fullness had now been released by the death and resurrection of Jesus; for of course every Jew knew perfectly well that there was a Holy Spirit. Accordingly they were instructed not about the Holy Spirit but about Jesus (19:4), baptized into His Name, and promptly - just as Paul had laid his hands upon them as part of the baptismal rite - received the gift of the Spirit with tongues and prophecy.

The purpose of these special "extensions" of Pentecost no doubt was to overcome the deep-seated Jewish prejudice against Samaritans and Gentiles, and to demonstrate that the One Baptism into the One Lord and the One Faith makes all equally One Body in One Spirit (Eph. 4:4-5). And the case of the Ephesians pointedly teaches the full glory of post-Pentecost Christian Baptism as distinct from the provisional incompleteness of John's pre-Pentecost baptism. Our own missionary work must, far from denigrating the Baptism of the unchurched but baptized multitudes of our land, make clear to them how precious is the treasure of Christianity which was offered them in their Baptism, and call on them to reclaim the gift by repentance and faith.

The whole point of Acts is not to separate but to connect Baptism and the Spirit, so that "Henceforth, baptism is Pentecost ... The initial Pentecost event did not institute replicas, it instituted Christian preaching and baptism. It is not little Pentecosts that are either here recorded or are in Acts intended to follow the one Pentecost. Pentecost endows the church with Word and Sacrament ... baptism is the Spirit's own sufficient evidence." (21) At the same time, as John 3 teaches,

> The descent of the Spirit in baptism remains a sovereign mystery and a wonder of grace. The only connection made for the Holy Spirit in this passage is with water. But how he relates himself to this water (coming immediately before, during, after?), or how or why he comes at all, is forbidden a too curious enquiry. (22)

By degrading the real, full Spirit-Baptism of the New Testament into a mere "water-baptism," and then hankering after something better, Pentecostalism ironically gets in its own way, or rather in the way of that true Spirit-fullness which comes not by human effort but as God's gift, alone through His appointed Gospel means. And Baptism offers it all!

F. Eucharist

St. Paul's two great chapters on the Lord's Supper (I Cor. 10-11) immediately precede his three-chapter tract on spiritual gifts. The connection is obvious. The Holy Supper is the normal "centre of gravity" of congregational worship - it is the acting out of the New Covenant - and of the One Body (I Cor. 10:17)! And it is in the congregational coming-together, which as a matter of course regularly includes the Sacrament (Acts 20:7 ff.), that the priesthood of believers, and such gifts as we have, are especially to be exercised. From this central fountain all the rest of church life and work is watered and fructified. To think that liturgical worship, centering in the Eucharist, must be stiff and regimented, is a complete misunderstanding of the Liturgy. Of the very liturgical Greek Orthodox Church C.S. Lewis writes:

> What pleased me most about a Greek Orthodox mass I once attended was that there seemed to be no prescribed behavior for the congregation. Some stood, some knelt, some sat, some walked; one crawled about the floor like a caterpillar. And the beauty of it was that no-

105

body took the slightest notice of what anyone else was doing. (23)

The essence of the Liturgy is not formality or parade-drill precision. It is the celebration of the Risen Saviour Who comes to share Himself and His life with His People in His Word and in the mystery of His Sacramental Presence. The deeper and richer our understanding of the Sacrament, the less cramped and narrow will be our understanding of the Liturgy. And then we will not experience informality, spontaneity, sharing, discussion, and the kind of church "business" that must have gone on in the Acts 20 Liturgy, as a threat to proper decorum and reverence. Indeed, why not adult Bible study, discussion, dialogue, even "business", not in place of the Sermon, but in addition to it, perhaps while the children are in Sunday School, yet as part of the one Service, concluding with the Sacrament?

At any rate, the Sacrament belongs in a setting suggesting festive release and Spirit-fruit like love and joy, rather than the gloom of unrelieved penitence, sadness, and even fear. (And the Sermon has a lot to do with the nature of this setting!) Yet sometimes one almost gets the impression that the Sacrament, like X-rays, must be taken in small doses and not too often, to avoid damage to our soul-tissue! No! The Sacrament is a gift of life, not a reward for already having it, say, through "proper preparation"! It is Christ's healing touch for sin-sick bodies and souls. Especially today when much of nominal Lutheranism is negotiating various surrenders of the Real Presence, a thorough study of the Biblical-Confessional teaching about the Sacrament - especially Augsburg Confession and Apology to and 24, the Large Catechism, and Formula of Concord, Art. 7 - could lead to great blessings, and might even close some credibility-gaps in our church life!

Of Pentecostal services Bruner writes: **"The Openness of Heaven . .** . . . The natural is in constant intersection with the supernatural and in constant susceptibility of being swallowed up by it . . . There is a sense in the Pentecostal meeting that the divine is not only (as in our churches) an object of worship but that he is also, and especially, a subject of action." (24).

Is it not precisely the Real Presence, rather than any ecstasies or "special effects", which is especially intended as that "openness of heaven," that divine human "intersection," for us presently Christians who have not seen and yet believe (John 20: 29)?

Concerning religious "enthusiasm" ("God-within") Msgr. Ronald Knox wrote:

"Fanaticism feels it knows not what; faith knows what it does not feel"! And Chesterton noted that "of all false religions the worst is the worship of the God within. For that Jones shall worship the God within, ultimately turns out to mean that Jones shall worship Jones".

Oddly enough the Pentecostal "theology of glory" huffs and puffs about inner strivings and exalted spirituality - and ends with externals: tongues!

The "theology of the Cross" sticks faithfully to humble outward means - and is granted the most precious of inner treasures: divine love! Baptism, preaching, Absolution, the Lord's Body and Blood - here alone Spirit-fullness is distributed.

Here is the place of hope and renewal. To devise more and other way makes not for a fuller but for an emptier gospel, and has always led to mischief and disaster:

> All this is the old devil and the old serpent who made enthusiasts of Adam and Eve. He led them from the external Word of God to spiritualizing and to their own imaginations, and he did this through other external words . ... in short, enthusiasm clings to Adam and his descendants from the beginning to the end of the world. It is a poison implanted and inoculated in man by the old dragon, and it is the source, strength, and power of all heresy, including that of the papacy and Mohammedanism. Accordingly, we should and must constantly maintain that God will not deal with us except through His external Word and Sacrament. Whatever is attributed to the Spirit apart from such Word and Sacrament is of the devil (Smalcald Articles, III/VIII, 5-10).

Footnotes

1 Bruner, op. cit., p. 290.

2 *ibid.*, p. 293.

3 *ibid.*, pp. 286-287.

4 John L. Sherrill, *They Speak With Other Tongues* (London: Hodder and Stoughton, 1967), pp. 110-111.

5 *ibid.*, p. 84.

6 Carroll Stegall Jr., *The Modern Tongues and Healing Movement* (Sydney: Open Air Campaigners, no date).

7 D. Vaughan Rees, *The 'Jesus Family' In Communist China* (Exeter: Paternoster Press, 1967), p. 78.

8 *ibid.*, p. 79.

9 Kurt Koch, *The Revival in Indonesia* (Evangelization Publishers, Western Germany, 1972), p. 263.

10 quoted in Bruner, op. cit., p. 297.

11 *ibid.*, pp. 301-302.

12 M. Darrol Bryant, *A World Broken By Unshared Bread* (Geneva: Lutheran World Federation and World Council of Churches, 1970), p.13.

13 Bruner, *op. cit.*, p. 299, n. 22.

14 Koch, *Indonesia*, pp. 263-266.

15 Bruner, *op. cit.* , p. 149.

16 *ibid.*, p. 301.

17 *ibid.*, pp. 244-245.

18 *ibid.*, p. 239.

19 Rousas Rushdoony, *Intellectual Schizophrenia* (Philadelphia: Presbyterian and Reformed Publishing Co., 1971), p. 121.

20 Whittaker Chambers, *Witness* (New York: Random House, 1952), p.9.

21 Bruner, *op. cit.,* pp. 169-170.

22 *ibid.*, p. 258.

23 C.S. Lewis, *Letters to Malcolm* (London: Fontana, 1964), p. 12.

24 Bruner, *op. cit.*, p. 137 .

1. Today the most basic Christian certainties are ____.
2. Pentecostalism tends to think of the gifts of the spirit as ____.
3. The Spirit's gifts are free gifts of ____.
4. The first and noblest gift of the Spirit is ____.
5. The gifts should be used for ____.
6. God loves a ____ giver.
7. The early Church took up special offerings for ____ but not for all ____.
8. The "Spirit Baptism" is marked by ____.
9. Ecstatic speech is quite typical of ____.
10. John Sherril reports that in 1955, the ____ were speaking in tongues.
11. Linguistic analysis of typical "tongues" show that they do not resemble ____.
12. Ecstatic speech of "tongues" may be ____.
13. The great fault of Pentecostal mission work is that ____.
14. The ark of Noah must be seen as a picture of our own ____.
15. Scripture interpretation must not come to rest in mere remainders of what happened ____ but must also ____.
16. According to Francis Schaeffer, what has infected our whole culture? ____.
17. The Ten Commandments have come ten ____.
18. It is the pastor's first duty to ____.
19. What did Whitaker Chambers write? ____.
20. What kind of labor does the Church need today? ____.
21. What fits the anti-rational temper of our times? ____.
22. The New Testament teaches only ____ Baptism.
23. Baptism actually ____.
24. The "tongues" of Pentecost were not gibberish but ____.
25. The Holy Supper is the ____.
26. The essence of the Liturgy is ____.

MARQUART'S WORKS

VOL. I
POPULAR WRITINGS

VOL. II
COMMUNISM

VOL. III
CHURCH AND MINISTRY

VOL. IV
APOLOGETICS

VOL. V
CHRISTENDOM

VOL. VI
JUSTIFICATION

VOL. VII
WORSHIP – LITURGY

VOL. VIII
BIBLE – HISTORICAL CRITICISM

VOL. IX
LUTHERANS

VOL. X
PERSON – (A TWENTY-FIRST CENTURY REFORMATION)

INDEX

110

111

Wilkerson, David – 98
Wisconsin Evangelical Lutheran
Synod (WELS) – 55-56, 59
Word – 10
World – 16
World Council of Churches (WCC)
– 1, 4, 30, 32, 61
World Relief – 94
Worship – 19,
Youth – 35, 45

Zwingli-Calvinist – 56